Brave Hearts

Pickthall and Philby

Two English Muslims in a Changing World

M A Sherif

IBT
Islamic Book Trust
Kuala Lumpur

Published 2011 by
Islamic Book Trust
607 Mutiara Majestic
Jalan Othman
46000 Petaling Jaya
Selangor, Malaysia
www.ibtbooks.com

Islamic Book Trust is affiliated with The Other Press.

Perpustakaan Negara Malaysia Cataloguing-in-Publication Data

Sherif, M. A., 1950-
Brave hearts : Pickthall and Philby two English muslims in a changing world / M A Sherif.
ISBN 978-967-5062-74-2
1. Philby, H. St. J. B. (Harry St. John Bridger), 1885-1960.
2. Pickthall, Marmaduke William, 1875-1936. 3. Scholars, Muslim --Europe. 4. Muslim converts--Europe. 5. Islam--Europe. I. Title.
297.092

Printed by
Academe Art and Printing Services Sdn Bhd
7, Jalan Rajawali 1A
Bandar Baru Puchong
Batu 8, Jalan Puchong
47100 Selangor

OCCASIONAL PAPER SERIES

Number 3

The purpose of this series is to bring to the public select essays on contemporary issues that have a relevance to Muslims. It covers a broad range of topics and serves to help readers understand current debates in the Muslim world through scholarly essays, working papers and research studies by renowned scholars from around the world.

The other title in this series are

The Qur'an, Orientalism and the *Encyclopaedia of the Qur'an*
by Muzaffar Iqbal

Why an Islamic State
The Life Projects of Two Great European Muslims
by M A Sherif

For more information, please visit *www.ibtbooks.com*

Brave Hearts
Pickthall and Philby
Two English Muslims in a Changing World

M A Sherif

At the turn of the last century, two remarkable Englishmen stood poised at the threshold of glittering careers. Pickthall, educated at Harrow where he was a contemporary of Winston Churchill, published a best-selling novel in 1903 set in the Levant, 'Saïd the Fisherman'. A few years later, Harry St. John Philby traversed the gilded path from Westminster School to Trinity College, Cambridge, where he had obtained a first, to take up an appointment in the Punjab in the Indian Civil Service (ICS). In the class-based milieu of Edwardian England, their trajectories were more or less pre-ordained, one perhaps becoming editor of *The Times*, and the other another star colonial administrator like Lord Malcolm Hailey. However, this was not to be.

Their travels in young adulthood brought them in contact with Muslim society and their own capacity for friendship fostered many mutual endearments. Something of Islam settled within their personalities and outlook, even though it would only be many years later that a formal declaration of the faith was to come—for Pickthall in 1917 at the age of 42, while Philby took the step in 1930, aged 45.

In tandem with their awareness of the Muslim way of life and values came a sense of disquiet with the conduct and policies of the British governments of the day. Their instincts prompted them to become vocal critics. Even though Pickthall was rooted in Somerset life and culture, while Philby clubbed at the Athenaeum, the Establishment could not accommodate their dissent. The issues they came to espouse—Pickthall's support for Ottoman Turkey prior to and after the Great War (1914-18), and Philby's concern for genuine Arab independence—challenged too many hegemonic interests. Their endeavours should not to be forgotten.

In most Muslim circles today, Muhammad Marmaduke Pickthall is perhaps only known for his translation of the Qur'an, while Abdullah Philby's name will most likely draw a blank. Pickthall's biographer Peter Clark provides a sympathetic account, though one coloured by the Armenian controversy, finding his subject to have "utter insensitivity" to this community's experiences.[1] A perceptive essay by Abdal Hakim Murad links Pickthall with the nineteenth century English tradition of dissent,[2] while another examines his loss of faith in Christianity to which he once deeply adhered.[3] Philby's life has been studied by Elizabeth Monroe, and in comparison with the saintly Pickthall, he emerges as a tough and irascible personality who developed a close friendship with Abdul Aziz ibn Saud and became a distinguished explorer-archaeologist discovering Sabean and Thamudic ruins in Arabia.[4] Monroe suggests that Philby's religious commitment was expedient, which is a simplistic assessment. Today Philby is mainly cited in discussions on the history of the Saudi oil concessions or in references to his son, Kim Philby, a member of the Cambridge spy ring that served Soviet interests during and after World War II.

There have been few attempts to draw together the experiences of these near-contemporaries to obtain a perspective of Muslim society at the turn of the last century, even though there were many clues on offer. Among common friends was Lady Zainab Cobbold, famous for her attempt to coax Pickthall to declare his Islam in 1914 over lunch at Claridges, and whom Philby later helped immensely when she performed the Hajj.[5] Lady Zaynab's celebrated account of the pilgrimage was published the following year, receiving a warm endorsement from Pickthall.[6] The literary critic Ethel Mannin included both Pickthall and Philby in her psychological study of writers, noting that "all he [Philby] wanted was peace and solitude."[7] T. E. Lawrence, the British army Intelligence officer who fanned the Arab revolt in the Hejaz against the Ottomans in 1917, cast a shadow on both their paths. For Pickthall, writing in 1935 shortly after Lawrence's death in a motor cycling accident, Lawrence's arguments in favour of Arab nationalism were "feeble and also insincere", though he was also "undoubtedly a man of talent in his way". [8] Philby was more appreciative, acknowledging Lawrence's genius, but noting: "if Lawrence's political judgement was often at fault, he was not alone in his error. The important thing is that he succeeded in making everyone who mattered believe that his solution was the right one…they all, in one way or other, gave him their support for placing the destinies of the Arab world at the mercy of the Hashemite dynasty."[9]

Pickthall and Philby were eye-witness to immense social and political changes in Muslim societies. They were also very different personalities, and an interleaving of their experiences conveys some of the twists and turns of the recent historical past, particularly in the face of a 'new world order' imposed on us in the aftermath of the Ottoman defeat in 1918.

Four themes have been taken up in this composite view of their lives:

- the sense of *enchantment* with Muslim life and character, and its personal impact

- the gradual process of *dissent* with the prevailing policies of the British government in Muslim lands
- their journeys of *relocation*, both in a physical and spiritual sense, with its ambiguities, certainties and enigmas
- their *analyses* of the Muslim predicament and hopes for the future

Discussions of Muslims in Britain are too often framed around 1950s immigration with a first generation wedded to a 'myth of return' until eventually reconciling themselves to a new terrain. The experiences of Pickthall and Philby are important because they offer a different narrative, that of indigenous Englishmen, products of Edwardian Britain, who discovered Islam and flourished within a Muslim camaraderie.

Enchantment

In 1894 while still in his teens, and with a sense of disappointment at being unable to take up his careers of choice, Pickthall embarked on a three-year long liberating voyage traversing Egypt, Turkey and the Levant (a term no longer used, but which would refer to *bilād al-Shām,* covering what is today Syria, Lebanon and Palestine including Jerusalem). He described the situation frankly, "I was eighteen years old, and, having failed in one or two adventures, I thought myself an all-round failure, and was much depressed. I dreamed of Eastern sunshine, palm trees, camels, desert sand, as of a Paradise which I had lost by my shortcomings. What was my rapture when my mother one fine day suggested that it might be good for me to travel in the East, because my longing for it seemed to indicate a natural instinct, with which she herself, possessing Eastern memories, was in full sympathy!"[10]

There was already something in his character which did

not conform to the typical Englishman: "All my education until then had tended to impose on me the cult of the thing done habitually upon a certain plane of our society. To seek to mix on equality with Orientals, of whatever breeding, was one of those things which was never done, nor even contemplated, by the kind of person who had been my model". By good fortune he fell in with

> a clever dragoman and one of the most famous jokers in all Syria, who happened to be lodging at my little hostelry, with nothing in the world to do but stare about him. He helped me to throw off the European and plunge into the native way of living. With him I rode about the plain of Sharon, sojourning among the fellâhîn and sitting in the coffee-shops of Ramleh, Lydda, Gaza, meeting all sorts of people, and acquiring the vernacular without an effort, in the manner of amusement. From dawn to sunset we were in the saddle.[11]

This familiarity raised eye-brows, particularly when he returned to the English colonial set in Jerusalem: "…it was in semi-native garb and with a love for Arabs which I was made to understand was hardly decent. My native friends were objects of suspicion. I was told that they were undesirable, and, when I stood up for them, was soon put down by the retort that I was very young."[12]

Pickthall responded to life in ancient Muslim cities like Cairo or Aleppo with a palpable sense of pleasure: "What struck me, even in its decay and poverty, was the joyousness of that life compared with anything that I had seen in Europe. The people seemed quite independent of our cares of life, our anxious clutching after wealth, our fear of death."[13] His encounter with the Shaykh of the great mosque in Damascus is well-known: Pickthall expressed his desire to become Muslim, but the Shaykh told him to wait till he had consulted his mother and was older.

The young traveller with a capacity for friendship came across Muslims who spoke to him with directness:

> "I had the fortune to know one Darfuri pretty intimately in my youth", Pickthall later recounted, "before I aspired to study the Qur'an. He told me once about this punishment for theft [severing of the hand] in his own country and I was shocked. 'How would you like', I said, 'to have your hand cut off?' 'If I became that shameful thing, a thief', he said, 'I should not be content with one hand only. They could cut off my head as well'."[14]

Pickthall returned home and soon made his mark as a novelist. His view of the novel was that it should not be "lies", but rather "by selection from the facts of life, drive[s] home some truths of real importance."[15] He achieved success with 'Saïd, the Fisherman'.

Even by 1903, at the age of 28, Pickthall was not unaware of Western designs on Ottoman lands. In a passage referring to the Ottoman-appointed governor of Damascus, a character in the 'Saïd' exclaims:

> Who is the governor of Damascus Sham?—and you tell me, His Excellency, Ahmed Basha, his honour, the Waly. I say no! and again no! Ahmed Basha—may Allah preserve him!—and all who bear rightful authority over us are but the servants of the Franks....Behold they gather upon us like vultures, they contend which shall have greatest share of the spoil—that is, of the wealth of Islam. Woe is me, for the end of all things draws nigh! The cross is set above the crescent, the feet above the head. If any oppose them they cry aloud to their masters, the powers of Europe, and great ships are sent across the sea to lay waste to our coasts... [16]

Pickthall visited Egypt again in 1907 and Ottoman Turkey in 1913. In the introduction to his 'With the Turk in Wartime' he wrote: "...I made up my mind to go to Turkey for a few months in order to escape an atmosphere that sickened me. The English press and public had, in this twentieth century, responded with fanaticism to the cry of a crusade against the Turk ...the solidarity of Christendom against a Muslim power was reckoned a fine thing by many people, but it broke the heart of Englishmen who loved the East."[17]

Residing in the Erenköy suburb of Istanbul, it felt like homecoming: "Real Eastern cries were wafted from the distant roadway. I felt entirely comfortable and in place for the first time since leaving my own Sussex farmhouse."[18] He wrote tender letters to his wife who had yet to join him: "...I am looking at everything with a view of showing it to you later. You will come in the very best season when the weather is set and fair and there will be flowers and fruits galore. I am certain that you have never seen a city half so beautiful, or any country so majestic as that on both sides of the Bosphorus. The minarets and domes are most imposing. One cannot help hoping that they may long remain."[19]

In another letter he wrote to her that he had taken to wearing a fez, "not a hat" and that "I shall have one of those mantilla kind of hats made for you—in white—like the Turkish ladies wear". He wrote to her that there was something "extraordinarily sweet and gentle" about the Turks: "I am quite sure that you will fall in love with the whole race."[20]

In the Ottoman Turkey of that period, the powers of the veteran Sultan Abdul Hamid II had been curtailed by a coalition of constitutional reformers, sometimes referred to as the *hürriyetperver*, and adherents of the Committee of Union and Progress (CUP), *Ittehat ve Terakki*. The new regime was unable to find a period of peace and stability to implement its policies and faced continuous external threats, including the Turko-Italian and Serbo-Bulgarian conflicts of 1911-1913 as well as criticisms from Western powers of the rights of Christian minorities.[21]

Pickthall soon had many friends prominent in public life. He was received by Refaat Bey of the CUP—"my most confidential friend in Turkey."[22] Pickthall also met Prince S'aid Halim, the foreign minister and future grand vizier, a man of letters and versatile linguist.[23] He had an interview with Talaat Pasha, a hero of the Bulgarian campaign and also prominent member of the CUP:

> One day I said to Talaat Bey: you always go about and move here and there without even a personal guard. You should have guards to defend you against all sudden and unexpected attacks. Talaat Bey, a famous Turk Muslim leader replied: 'There is no better Guardian than Almighty Allah'. This experience strengthened my belief in Allah. I understood from Talaat Bey that according to Islamic belief death cannot anticipate or fall behind its fixed time. Hence this unusual courage seemed to me very strange in the beginning.[24]

Pickthall expressed his wish to Talaat to enter the fold of Islam. The General responded much like the venerable Damascene sheikh, advising him to bide his time.

Pickthall's access to such high levels of Ottoman society was eased by the letters of introduction from his friend Aubrey Herbert and one Pangiris Bey in London, and possibly his own contacts with dissidents in exile like the scholar-diplomats AbdulHak Hamid and and Halil Halid.[25] However his personal charisma undoubtedly played a role.

Soon after his return to England, Pickthall emulated some of the CUP contacts in Istanbul and joined the Misericordia Lodge, "at the invitation of Dr Rosedale, DD."[26] Freemasonry at the time provided a fellowship that overcame barriers of race and class.[27]

❖

Philby arrived in India in 1909 at the age of 23 and his first posting in the Indian Civil Service was in the Jhelum district. Much like Pickthall, he possessed a natural talent for languages and soon picked up Urdu and Punjabi. His duties as a district officer required him to tour the country-side, acting as magistrate and adjudicating on taxes due to the Raj. His writing was far more down to earth than Pickthall's, and around 1910 he noted:

> The inhabitants of the Jhelum district as a whole are mainly Muslim, the famous Punjabi Mussalmans, who contribute so large a number of recruits to the Indian army; but considerable Hindu communities are to be found in the towns...while there are also some Hindu villages whose identity was always easily ascertainable owing to their ladies' habit of bathing naked and unashamed at the village wells, generally by the roadside. This no doubt saved them the labour of carrying their bath-water up to their homes, as the Muslim women, more concerned for privacy, had to do. This composition of the local population gave one a good cross-section of Indian life for study, although from the beginning it was rather the Muslim than the Hindu culture that attracted and interested me. At an early stage I began reading the Qur'an with my junior court clerk, Muhiy-al-din, under whose guidance also I often explored the town and bazaar, besides attending the periodic festivals, visiting the local mosques and the like.[28]

Elsewhere, Philby wrote that "ever since my early days in India I had been greatly attracted by Islam and its highly simplified emphasis on what seemed to me the eternal verities of life and philosophy."[29]

Five years later, in 1915, by which time he had also mastered Arabic, Philby was transferred to Mesopotamia. Initially he served as a translator and civilian administrator in the political office of Sir Percy Cox. The British colonial officers in India deemed the regions of Basra and Bahrain to fall within their orbit, and with the outbreak of World War I in 1914, large numbers of Indian troops were despatched to fight the Ottomans and secure the oil fields. By 1917 Philby was travelling in the Nejdi desert, charged with sounding out Abdul Aziz ibn Saud and encouraging him to harass the Turks. Much like Pickthall's enchantment with the Turks, Philby noted, "I had fallen in love with Arabia."[30]

The ways and customs of Muslims were often unavoidable and stopped Philby in his tracks, quite literally:

> ...it was an intolerable affront to pass through a village or a Badawin encampment in the desert without claiming the hospitality of its occupants; I was once fired on from and made to return to Madaba in Trans-Jordan when I committed this crime, being in a hurry to reach Amman...the foundation of society in those days was virtue itself, as defined by the Qur'an and the tradition of the Prophet.[31]

In another desert journey before he had entered the fold of Islam, Philby became annoyed by the stops for prayer and decided to show his displeasure with his guides by riding out alone. Apparently his camel rebelled, and galloped him back and deposited him beside the line of men in prayer![32]

Philby was captivated by the Nejdis, later becoming their chieftain's outspoken advocate when the British and French set about dismembering the Ottoman's Arab provinces after World War I. He had praise for the old Wahhabi dispensation and its ways:

> ...It was not till I went to Arabia that I came into contact with what seemed to me undeniably a pure form of Islam, deriving exclusively from the original sources of inspiration, the Qur'an and the Traditions of the Prophet, and owing nothing to theological interpolation and exegesis. The Wahhabi creed seemed to me, as a result of deep study, to be the ideal form of

religion, and the fanaticism of its followers did not displease me. They had the merit of practising what they believed and preached, while their religion seemed admirably suited to the needs of human life and society in their simplest form. It was a religion which one could accept without intellectual dishonesty as a guide to life and conduct, and whose ethical standards seem to conform better than those of other religions—Christianity for instance—to the basic needs of humanity. If its code was severe in some respects, it refused to countenance bastardy, while it's often criticised system of polygamy provided a better safeguard against adultery and fornication than the Ten Commandments.[33]

Of Abdul Aziz ibn Saud, Philby would write that he was, "…constant, unchanging and unchangeable; simple to the end in his personal tastes and needs; devout and God-fearing beyond question, generous to a fault….the greatest Wahhabi, the like of whom will never be seen again."[34]

❖

Both Pickthall and Philby admired a glint of steel in the human character. A dramatic passage in 'Saïd the Fisherman' conveys the powerful personality of the Algerian *mujahid* Abd al-Qadir al-Jazairi, who resisted the French in Algeria but was defeated and exiled, arriving in Syria in 1855. Pickthall describes a scene, as witnessed by the character Saïd, in which Abd al-Qadir and his men come to the rescue of some nuns in Damascus:

The mob…set to work once more. "To the French convent! Someone shouted. "Let the nuns be ravished and then slain!" The cry was taken up on all hands with laughter and coarse jibes…those in front hammered at a strong door [of the convent]….All at once there was a backward movement. Another panic got hold of the crowd. A cry, "The soldiers!" was again raised….A small troop of armed men rode up to the door of the nunnery. They were seen plainly of all, towering as they did on horseback above the seething mass on foot. Most of them rode with their chargers at the foremost, who drew back in alarm; while a few, among whom was the leader, dismounted and entered the convent, the door of which was promptly opened to them.

A might roar went up from the multitude.

"It is Abdul Cader!"—"May Allah preserve his Grace!"—"He goes to take vengeance upon his enemies!"—"It was the French who wronged and imprisoned him, though he fought them brave as a lion!"—"He is come to claim all the French nuns for his harim!"—"Allah is just!"—"May all the Franks perish, and their women be dishonoured!"—"Long live the might of Islam!"—"May Allah preserve Abdul Cader, the glory of the Faith!"

But applause was turned to oaths and howls of rage when the hero and his officers reappeared, escorting with respect a train of black-robed nuns, each with the obnoxious cross shining on her bosom. The horsemen closed around them as a bodyguard; the leaders sprang to their saddles. Then the fury of the crowd broke all bounds. The coolness of the rescuers as they rode away had a point of contempt which stung the rout to madness....raging like a winter-torrent, the crowd surged forward in pursuit. The horsemen were constrained to a foot's pace, having regard for the women in their midst. The mob was close upon them. Stones and other missiles began to whiz through the air. Of a sudden the whole mass swayed back, every man jostling his neighbour.

Abdul Cader had turned his horse about and was sitting motionless, his eyes ranging sternly over the sea of turbaned heads and swarthy, malignant faces. A last stone, flung at random from the heart of the throng, struck his arm and made him wince. He raised his hand to his tarbush, commanding silence. An awe-stricken hush spread like a breath over the crowd. This man was the established idol of the populace. He was the greatest living hero of Islam, and at heart they gloried in his intrepidity.

"What is this, O my friends?" His voice rang out clear and measured. "Will you provoke the wrath of Allah against this city? Will you anger Him so that He turn away His face from us for ever? It has been told to you how I have fought for Islam—ay, and borne imprisonment and exile for our holy Faith. But I tell you I would rather be the meanest Christian slain this day in the sight of Allah than one of you whose hands are red with his blood. Shame on you, Muslimun! Shame on you, I say! Would to Allah I had gone to my grave ere ever this day dawned for the faith!"

He gazed for a moment, on the silent crowd; then, turning, set spurs to his horse and cantered away. But the foremost, among whom was Saïd, saw that his eyes glistened....[35]

In Saïd's description of Sidi Abdul Qader, Pickthall captured the Islamic value of *muruwwah* or honour. Philby was also alert to this, though in a very different type of incident he witnessed in 1917-1918:

> Soon after we had arrived in camp Ibn Saud rode in followed by the solid phalanx of his escort...the young princes, Faisal and Fahad, who had been left behind in camp here during the expedition, immediately came in with the kiss of welcome for their father on both sides of the nose and on top of it, and then took their places in the audience tent with becoming gravity. Ibn Saud enquired of their health in the most formal manner as if they were honoured strangers rather than his *own children* [Philby's italics] yet to reach their teens—no doubt part of the educational routine designed to teach manners and deportment by practice rather than precept.[36]

It was to Abdul Aziz ibn Saud that Philby turned to in 1924 when he wished to declare his Islam—at the age of 39. Much like the advice given to Pickthall, the chieftain asked him to defer the decision.[37]

Muslim society even under colonialism retained a vitality and integrity that could draw enquiring minds, whether someone of finesse like Pickthall, or the tough Philby. Their inner voice responded to a message even though they were lodged in the bosom of Empire, much like Āsiyah in the court of Pharoah.

Dissent

Around 1906 neither Englishman was particularly perturbed by an incident in Egypt near the village of Denshawi, when British army officers, out on a pigeon shoot, came into dispute with local villagers who were pigeon breeders. In the ensuing confrontation, an Egyptian woman and four men were peppered with shot. The fellahin responded with their wooden sticks, and one of the English officers—a Captain Bull—dashed off to bring help. However he suffered sunstroke, fell and passed away. A village tried to help him out, but in vain. Thinking the villager had killed him, Bull's comrades beat the man to death. No man was tried for this man's murder, but a court sentenced four peasants to public hanging, and others to life imprisonment or lashes.[38]

Pickthall's reaction to the incident was stock imperialist. His biographer Peter Clark states that Pickthall accepted the severity of the exemplary punishment, arguing that pigeon-breeders were the most turbulent among Egyptian villagers and that British justice was 'even-handed'.[39] At the time Philby was still at Oxford, where he spoke at the Union defending the sentences.[40] Pickthall or Philby did not express the anti-colonialist sentiments of say Wilfred Scawen Blunt, who supported the Egyptian nationalist awakening and led protest in Britain over the high-handedness and brutality at Denshawi. Pickthall's novel written after a sojourn in Egypt at this time, 'The Children of the Nile', was rich in social history but politically banal: "his Egyptian novel did not upset Pickthall's English hosts in Cairo."[41]

Pickthall's change of heart occurred sometime during his next visit to Egypt and Palestine two years later between September 1908 and May 1909. British policy makers, instead of welcoming the reforms initiated by the *hürriyetperver* and *Ittehat ve Terakki* coalition within Ottoman society at the time, reacted with hostility. For example Foreign Secretary Lord Grey noted:

> If Turkey really establishes a Constitution and keeps it on its feet, and becomes strong itself, the consequences will reach further than any of us can yet foresee. The effect in Egypt will be tremendous, and will make itself felt in India. Hitherto whenever we have had Mahometan subjects, we have been able to tell them that the subjects ruled by the head of their religion were under a despotism which was not a benevolent one; while our Mahometan subjects were under a despotism which was benevolent....[42]

Pickthall expected Britain to support the Ottoman reformers, and his trust in the 'even-handedness' of British justice was further shaken when Austria was allowed to incorporate Bosnia and Herzegovina within its territories even though legal right rested with the Ottomans.[43]

A counter-coup in support of Sultan Abdul Hamid II took place in April 1909 but it was unsuccessful, and in a brief period of confusion that followed before the CUP re-established its power and exiled Sultan Abdul Hamid, there were revolts by the Armenians in Adana. The suppression of this revolt prompted a wave of anti-Ottoman statements by British politicians, which also rankled with Pickthall, who had never been impressed by the Armenian character.[44] He would remain an ardent defender of the Ottoman stand on the Armenians, and later when writing about Adana, he noted:

> In the early spring of 1909, the arrogant and warlike attitude of the Armenian Revolutionaries in the vilayet of Adana and a discovery of bombs enraged the Muslim population and made them listen to the preaching of reactionary agents, who failed in every other province of the empire to provoke disorders. The result was a panic struggle ending in massacre.[45]

Pickthall knew first-hand the conditions of non-Muslim minorities in Muslim lands and could see through the western powers' campaigns to make this a central issue. The reality was that non-Muslims were privileged and benefited from concessions not available to ordinary Ottomans.[46]

During his visit to Istanbul in March 1913 Pickthall had been at pains to check for himself reports in the British media of the mistreatment of Europeans in Istanbul because of 'Ottoman fanaticism'. Pickthall found that "there is not, never has been any danger here for Europeans. The rumours current in the west are due to the reports of Armenians, Greeks and other Levantines..."[47]

He also obtained information on the treatment meted out to Muslims. He met Khalid Bey, "the chief wire puller of the Party of Union and Progress":

> I asked him the exact number of *mohajirin* (refugees) from Thrace and Macedonia who have come to Turkey. He went at once and telephoned the Sublime Porte. Within five minutes he was back beside me with the answer: 160,000 or more, not less...he also told me that among the refugees are hundreds of girls who have been violated by the Bulgars and hundreds of men who have been mutilated.[48]

The well-informed Pickthall and his friend, the MP Aubrey Herbert, were amongst the handful of British public figures that entered public debate in the defence of the Ottomans and challenged the accounts of minorities' persecutions. Following his visit to Istanbul in 1913, he returned an even more convinced and committed advocate of the Ottoman cause, culminating with his 'With the Turk in Wartime', cited earlier and published in 1914. The Old Harrovian now aligned himself with a group of anti-colonialist activists associated with the 'New Age' journal, including the pan-Africanist, pan-Islamist and part-Sudanese Dusé Mohamed Ali. The journal's contributors "included many of the liveliest minds of the time" while Dusé was an activist who, to the concern of British Intelligence, had collected funds in Britain in 1913 for the purchase of arms for Ottoman Arabs in the Turco-Italian wars.[49]

Another home truth soon dawned on Pickthall:

> ..when one hears (as I did lately) in an English church, the Turks compared to Satan, the Bulgarian advance to that of Christian souls assailing Paradise, one can only gasp. It was as if Muslim blood may be shed more lightly (they would not put it so, but it amounts to that).[50]

In November 1914, Britain and France formerly declared war on Ottoman Turkey. Pickthall did not desert his corner in the name of 'My country, right or wrong', and joined the Anglo-Ottoman Society and the Central Islamic Society. Dusé's offices at 158 Fleet Street in London were also the premises of the Islamic Society. The offices were raided by the police in December 1914, based on information received by MI5.[51] In addition Pickthall was "suspected of being an enemy agent ever since his return from Constantinople at the beginning of the war."[52] Pickthall was not to be intimidated, and was particularly active in challenging official and media accounts of further atrocities against Armenians.

In particular he responded to Arnold Toynbee, who headed a Section E at the Bureau of Intelligence at the Department of Information. Toynbee had published a piece of black propaganda—a pamphlet on 'atrocities' inflicted by the

Ottomans on Armenians. Pickthall described it as being based on "fanatical and altogether false assumptions."[53]

This was at the time policy makers were preparing the ground for the McMahon-Hussein Agreement in which Britain promised Sherif Hussein of Hejaz sovereignty of more or less the whole of the *Jazīrah al-'Arab* if he attacked the Ottomans!

Much to the Establishment's chagrin, Pickthall in February 1915 made public his remarkably prescient assessment on the real imperialist aims:

> Our unknown rulers seem so far as I can learn to contemplate a full partition of the Turkish Empire....England will have southern Mesopotamia and probably all the territory southward roughly of a line drawn on the map from a point little north of Samara on the Tigris to a point a little south of Jaffa on the Coast of Palestine. The whole peninsula of Arabia would be included in her 'sphere of influence' for gradual absorption. France will have much of Syria.[54]

To cap it all, Pickthall even launched a peace initiative to end the War, using the offices of his Masonic friend Dr Rosedale to contact Sir Maurice de Bunsen at the Foreign Office. The response was swift: "Mr Pickthall is most undesirable, and should in no way be encouraged. In fact he ought to be interned as an enemy alien."[55] The lynchpin policy maker Sir Mark Sykes, who was later to cut a secret deal with France for the partitioning of the Levant—the Sykes-Picot Agreement—admonished Pickthall severely: "I do not consider that it is proper that you should assume absolute friendship to an enemy State… and further speak in a distinctly hostile tone of your own government."[56]

Sykes was also emerging as a passionate supporter of Chaim Weizmann, lobbying in London for a Zionist entity in Palestine. The Zionists feared a peace deal with Turkey as it would derail their plans for an autonomous homeland in Palestine under

British supervision. The anti-Turks in British policy circles became proto-Zionists, much as a century later, the pro-'War on Terror' neo-Cons were also Israeli partisans.

There could not have been more of an Englishman than the Suffolk-imbued Pickthall, but with the high stakes of a new world order beckoning, even he could be regarded as an 'enemy alien' in his own land.[57]

Pickthall continued with his stand nevertheless. The Central Islamic Society—under the leadership of the Indian Muslim barrister and writer Mushir Hosain Kidwai—appointed him as its spokesperson on "Muslim interests in Palestine."[58] Alert to the growing support in Government for a declaration supporting a Jewish homeland, he spoke at a meeting of the Central Islamic Society in June 1917, several months prior to his public declaration of his Islamic faith:

> I should regard it as a disaster if that country [Palestine] should be taken from the Muslim government. Must even that sacred ground be exploited by the profiteer? Must cinema places and cafés-chantants be established in Jerusalem and harlots walk the Via Dolorosa? The Muslims have preserved Jerusalem as a holy city; Palestine is a holy country, with all reverence. Would modern Christians, modern Jews, have done the like… if you want to have a new and terrible storm-centre for the world, hand over Palestine to any Christian Power…the state of things will be made worse by conquest, rousing ambitions where the population is so mixed. Among the recent Jewish immigrants into Palestine—the Jews of the Zionist movement as distinct from the native Jews—there is an extreme and narrow fanaticism which their enlightened co-religionists in Europe hardly, I think, realise. They hate the Christian and they hate the Muslim: and their supremacy would mean oppression for the other elements of the population. Their avowed intention is to get possession of the Rock (the so-called Mosque of Omar) and the Mosque El Aksa, which is

> the second Holy Place of El Islam—because it was the site of their Temple...[59]

Pickthall persisted in the same vein at a meeting of the Independent Labour Party in August 1917, where his remarks were monitored by one Ormsby-Gore at the Foreign Office:

> ...even more extraordinary is the assertion that the disruption of the Young Turk Empire ... 'would do injustice to the Muslim population'. This is a truly amazing statement, such as we might expect from Mr Marmaduke Pickthall and similar anti-Semitic pro-Turks.[60]

The efforts of the Central Islamic Society and Pickthall were ignored by Government. Wiezmann's skilful lobbying led to the fateful day, 2nd November 1917, when the British Government approved the statement, now known as the Balfour Declaration. It stated His Majesty's Government "viewed with favour the establishment in Palestine of a national home for the Jewish people, and will use all its best endeavours to facilitate the achievement of this object..."

A few weeks later Pickthall was to finally publicly declare his entry to Islam at the age of 43, in the course of a lecture at the Muslim Literary Society in London. He was spell-binding in his speeches no less than in his writing. An observer at this meeting noted, "from start to finish, Pickthall held his audience as if in a spell by his erudition, by his deep-thinking and lastly by the most genuine and rock-like faith...when he sat down, everyone of his hearers felt that they had lived through during that one short hour the most remarkable period in his or her life."[61]

His estrangement with what Britain had come to stand for became more marked in 1918: "What Muslim ever came near to inventing poison gas, or building Dreadnoughts, or even dreamt of a gun with a range of more than 80 miles?"[62]

Pickthall was now under surveillance, with Intelligence

reports prepared on his activities:

> On 24.1.18 Marmaduke Pickthall delivered a lecture before the 'Cercle d'Etudes Ethnographiques' entitled 'A plea for Asia'. He condemned the 'Gladstonian Doctrine' of turning the Turk out of Europe, repudiated the Arab Movement, applauded the Turks' Pan-Turanian policy, ascribed the Armenian massacres to European intrigue, pleaded for the application of self-determination principle to Turkey…this speech is characteristic of the speeches and writings of this man…[63]

❖

Philby was active in a different theatre of operations during these years of World War I. Still in the Indian Civil Service and on secondment to Mesopotamia, he was assigned a sensitive political mission to coax Abdul Aziz ibn Saud to attack a fellow Nejdi, Ibn Rashid of Haïl, who was allied to the Ottomans.[64]

The British policy makers in Mesopotamia were loyal to the India Office in Delhi that had dreams of extending its reach. On the other hand, the Foreign Office's Arab Bureau based in Egypt dreamt of their own British Arab empire, centred in Cairo. The two regional policy centres often worked at cross-purposes, but London was well-aware and managed a grand strategy. While Sir Percy Cox at his headquarters in Basra was allowed to build alliances with ibn Saud in the Nejd, Sir Reginald Wingate in Cairo controlled agents like T. E. Lawrence sent to Sherif Hussein in the Hejaz to ferment rebellion against the Ottomans. These were the two wings of the 'Arab movement' cultivated by Britain under extremely intelligent and able Arabists adept at playing off the animosity between Sherif Hussein and Abdul Aziz Ibn Saud.[65]

Abdul Aziz ibn Saud, like Sherif Hussein in the Hejaz, was tempted with monies and arms. He was offered payments in gold, 1000 rifles and ammunition. A hitch however arose when the weapons, already transferred to his agent in Kuwait in October 1917, were impounded. This was much to Philby's distress, because it was a breach of promise and he was left high and dry facing Ibn Saud:

> I was thunderstruck and raged impotently. His Majesty's Government has decided that they no longer wanted Ibn Saud to proceed with the campaign against Haïl lest his success should ruffle the temper of King Hussain …for such a proceeding as the withdrawal of a gift already given there could be no excuse….I had no leg to stand on and nothing to reply….there was no doubt in my mind that His Majesty's Government, laying plans behind a smoke-screen of misrepresentation, had entered upon a course of error which could lead them into undreamed-of consequences…I could not accept as final or satisfactory the policy which I was instructed to communicate to Ibn Saud…..[66]

Some of the Arab *muruwwah* had rubbed off on Philby. Like in the case of Pickthall, once his confidence in the integrity of 'His Majesty's Government' was shaken, things could never be the same again.

After the War, the Sykes-Picot agreement was implemented, with Mesopotamia and neighbouring regions placed in the 'British zone'. This included the southern Levant, which was divided into two—Palestine and Transjordan. Sherif Hussein became 'King of Hejaz'—he was disabused of the title 'King of Arabia'—and the British cabinet endorsed Lawrence's proposals to reward Sherif Hussein's sons with kingdoms under the British mandate. The second son Abdullah was made Emir of Transjordan, while another younger son, Faisal ibn Hussain (not to be confused with Abdul Aziz ibn Saud's son also named Faisal), much to French chagrin, was foisted on Syria. However this was a short-lived affair and Faisal was then nominated to be ruler of Iraq after an election.

Philby, back in Baghdad and reporting to Sir Percy Cox again, disagreed with this policy: by his standards, the British government was installing a Hashemite puppet for its own imperial ends, and jettisoning the promises about the freedom of choice made in the Anglo-French Declaration[67]. Cox gave Philby the job of escorting Faisal from Basra, where he had arrived on a British warship, to Baghdad. Throughout the journey, Philby harangued Faisal:

> ...So far as the people in general have any policy, it sums up in one word—independence. The rebellion was led and fought on that single issue...if you intend to base your campaign on the fact that you are the accepted nominee of the British government, I think your chances are extremely slender...[68]

When Britain decided to dispense with elections and proclaimed Faisal ibn Hussein as King of Iraq in 1921—as Faisal I—Philby was ready to resign. Cox arranged for his transfer to Transjordan to provide administrative support to Emir Abdullah. Philby's task was to manage its finances, under the overall supervision of the Zionist Sir Herbert Samuel, who represented Britain as the mandatory power and served as head of the Palestinian administration.

It was in Transjordan that Philby encountered T.E. Lawrence, and his portrait hints at some of the dark deals of the day:

> ...it was undoubtedly Lawrence who made Faisal qualify for this prize [Iraq] by arranging the understanding with Dr Weizmann regarding the establishment of a national home for the Jews in Palestine....For a moment it seemed that his dream of a Sharifian cordon separating the ferocious Wahhabis of the Arabian desert from the civilised world had been realised; and the shock of the ignominious defeat of the Sharifian army by [Abdul Aziz] ibn Saud in May 1919 was light-heartedly absorbed by him in a sense of almost personal

> triumph over the obstinate old King Hussain who had always, and quite openly, opposed his plans for the establishment of Faisal as independent monarch...Lawrence's mission to Jedda [to conclude an Anglo-Hejazi treaty] was a failure, as King Hussein resolutely refused to accord any kind of recognition to the Jewish National Home…the Lawrence dream of Sharifian domination in all Arabia had been shattered by Ibn Saud.[69]

As in Iraq, Philby pressed for Arab autonomy in Transjordan, and was riled by incidents that put it at risk:

> Philby had always held that the pilgrim railway, originally built in Turkish times with contributions from the faithful, ought to be managed by a Muslim board with its seat at Madina. The mandatory powers thought differently and had placed it under a board of control consisting of British, French and Hijazi representatives. Philby, incensed because the Transjordan sector was run by the Palestine Railways, early in 1924 arbitrarily and unilaterally handed over control of the sector to King Hussein's eldest son Ali, at the time on a visit to Amman.[70]

Relationships with Samuel worsened:

> I had set the country on the high road to effective independence which with patience could have developed on sound lines, had not Sir Herbert Samuel and the Palestine Government found such developments inconsistent with their ultimate aims…[71]

Eventually in January 1924 Philby felt he had to act:

> I have resigned this job for many, very many reasons; the chief of them is that I can no longer go on working with the present High Commissioner who, being a Zionist Jew, cannot hold the scales even between Zionist and Arab interests. Besides this, Abdullah has rather let me down by his personal extravagance which is on such a scale that he is simply inviting interference, and getting it in full measure from HMG, which means the Zionist element. So I am off.[72]

It was perhaps in this mutinous mood that Philby ventured on a peace mission in the Hejaz. In September 1924, Abdul Aziz Ibn Saud, styling himself as Sultan of Nejd, started his military campaign against Sherif Hussein in the Hejaz. Hussein stepped down the following month, and was succeeded by his son Ali. Without seeking approval from his superiors, Philby landed in Jedda and offered to negotiate between Ali and Ibn Saud. The British Consul in Jedda told him that his movements would be restricted to Jedda, and that the 'normal sequel' of ignoring government orders was dismissal. Philby described his conversation with the Consul, Reader Bullard:

> How could such restriction be reconciled with the declared neutrality of the British Government, or with their apparent acquiescence of the Indian Caliphate Committee, whose delegation was openly proclaiming its intention to work against the interests of the Sharifian dynasty, which it regarded as a creature of British imperialism? 'Oh, but they are Muslims', replied Bullard. 'Well, what if I too turn Muslim? It would be better for me to be that then regarded as a Christian'....I protested that the British Government had no moral right to prevent efforts to save the Hejaz from an orgy of bloodshed, occasioned by its own misguided policy in the past, and that in particular it was very mean on its part to use against me the only weapon that they could use with effect, namely the threat of my pension and reduce my family to penury. I could not take that risk, as it knew all too well; but I would yet have my revenge.[73]

When Abdul Aziz Ibn Saud's forces started shelling Jedda, Philby observed with relish that the first shell landed on Bullard's bed, "after he had risen to dress, and it failed to explode". Fearing the blood bath that Ibn Saud's Ikhwan militia had earlier perpetrated in Taif, Ali fled to his brother Faisal I in Iraq after receiving an ultimatum.[74]

Philby came off the Government's payroll in January 1925. His decision to resign was a bold act for someone with no income except for thirteen years' purchase of his ICS pension. He wrote a series of newspaper and journal articles on the situation in Hejaz, describing Ibn Saud's capture of Mecca and the siege of Medina and voicing criticism of Britain's annexation of the Aqaba-Maan region, removing it from the Hejaz for incorporation into Transjordan, Philby described this as "an act of aggression against a weak state."[75]

Following Balfour's visit to Palestine to inaugurate the Hebrew University in April 1925, Philby exposed the underhand way the ground was prepared for a Zionist enclave following the Balfour Declaration:

> ...the Arabs of Palestine...maintained consistently and unswervingly an attitude of dignified protest against the unwelcome visit to their country of one who is publicly and peculiarly identified with an act of betrayal for whose parallel—the shekels and the kiss and all the rest of it—we have to go back to the Gardens of Gethsemane....
>
> We shall never be allowed to know the exact nature of the negotiations with the Zionist leaders which preceded the Balfour Declaration in November 1917 or the exact terms of the bargain for which the quid pro quo was the establishment of the Jewish domination in Palestine. But surely it is unworthy of the British Government to take refuge behind the rest of the civilised world and the League of Nations and to shuffle off on to them a responsibility which rests justly on no one but itself!
>
> It is absurd, at any rate to suggest that the civilised world as a whole approves of the Zionist policy except in so far as it constitutes a future embarrassment to Great Britain, or that it views that policy as anything but an instrument of British imperialism.
>
> ...the conditions of the Mandate were drawn up by His

> Majesty's Government in consultation with the Zionists, and that the League of Nations had nothing to do with them except to approve of them when invited to do so: that was necessary to give them validity in the eyes of international law....the whole business of the 'A' mandates [applying to former Ottoman territories] in general, and of the Palestine in particular, is humbug writ large....
>
> Why make a difference between...the promises of Balfour and those of McMahon? The reason is obvious but may be stated here. The British Government has not the slightest intention of keeping promises to Arabs, and have every intention of implementing its promises to the Jews if it can...[76]

Philby's article was immediately criticised by the Zionist lobby in Britain, with one Israel Cohen, a future long-serving general secretary of the 'Zionist Organisation in UK' labelling it an "intemperate philippic."[77] Philby's well-wishers offered him some warnings:

> This is not an alarm trumpet, but a call to carefulness and extreme watchfulness. You are in danger...you have to make up your mind to combat very seriously those enemies of the Arabs who are so active that one of them, I am told, spent in a single year one hundred million francs in local propaganda...[78]

Relocations

Towards the end of the war Pickthall was conscripted to the army as a private till discharged in March 1919. The experience seems to have helped him decide what to do next. "It is certain that I have wasted the greater part of my life", he declared in one of his *khuṭbahs* of this period, adding

> that I have done no good that I should care to show before the Lord of goodness, yet I am no longer afraid to stand before Him at the Judgement Day, because I have surrendered to His Will.[79]

He also drew a moral lesson from the barrack rooms:

> Class distinctions are not absent from Muslim brotherhood, but class prejudices are. There is free speech and free intercourse between all sorts and conditions of men, and between all sorts and conditions of women. Those prejudices mar the outlook of most English people...one of the greatest blessings which Islam brings to an Englishman is the deliverance from this insanity. His vision grows serene, enabling him to smile at the pretentions of all parties, to accept men on their merits, with a brotherly regard for men whose conduct pleases him. Irrespective of colour or race or colour, I have just been in the British army in the ranks—pitch forked, so to speak, at forty-three, among all sorts of men—and I have found this Muslim point of view a godsend, making me content where once I should have been extremely miserable.[80]

He then took up employment at the London-based 'Islamic Information Bureau' associated with two Indian Muslims, Mushir Hussain Kidwai and the businessman, *Nazim-ut-tujar* Haji M. Hashim Ispahani. The Intelligence reports of the day—with a touch of paranoia—placed him in a leadership role:

> The Islamic Information Bureau, at first known as the Islamic Defence League, was formed in July 1919. Its chief promoters were Marmaduke Pickthall, with whom the idea originated, M.H. Kidwai, of the Mosque, Woking, and Mirza H. Ispahani of 21 Mincing Lane, EC...the object was to form an information bureau (on the lines of the People's Russian Information Bureau) for the collection and circulation of all Islamic news...the Bureau would be to all appearances above suspicion. Information would be obtained from all Muslim countries, and from non-Muslim countries where Muslims live, for organising a Muslim intelligence service to operate from London and it was hoped that the Bureau would become 'the power behind the scenes' in all Islamic affairs. It would work in support of the Anglo-Ottoman Society, the League of Justice for Asia and Africa, the Islamic Society and all other

> bodies working in support of Islam but was not intended to supplant them....Marmaduke Pickthall, an author and noted pro-Turk, was appointed Hon. Sec. receiving only pocket expenses....[81]

The Muslims of the sub-continent, having lost political authority in their own homeland, felt honour-bound to preserve the might of the Ottoman caliphate. They were of course unknowing of the Sykes-Picot understanding or other secret agreements and were shocked to discover that the post-war Peace Conferences were dismembering Ottoman lands—including Palestine, the *jazīrah al-'Arab* (Arabian peninsula) and Mesopotamia—thus rendered the caliphate ineffectual as a world power. All that the Indian Khilafatist movement could now do was to remind Britain of her pledges made to the Muslims of India at the outbreak of World War I.[82] The Islamic Information Bureau in London served as the Khilafatist movement's base, providing support to the visiting Indian delegations led by Maulana Mohamed Ali Jauhar.

In October 1919 Pickthall chaired a 'Day of Prayer for the Khalifa' in London. He also continued to confront the Armenian lobby in Britain, writing to them in the same month in response to their widely circulated statement claiming that Islam condoned the 'killing at sight' of Christians. Writing on behalf of the Islamic Information Bureau, Pickthall asked, "in the name of 150,000,000 British subjects, whose religion they misrepresent, kindly to give me chapter and verse of the Koran" on which they base their statement.[83] Pickthall's challenge demanded some courage: Armenians had vowed vengeance in Europe, and were soon to fulfil this threat by assassinating two of his acquaintances, Talaat Pasha and Prince S'aid Halim.

The Islamic Information Bureau also commenced publishing a monthly paper, 'Muslim Outlook', during his tenure. However

Pickthall did not find the institutional environment congenial, writing to Aubrey Herbert towards the end of 1919:

> With regard to the Bureau, of which I am unworthy secretary, I hope you did not think me insensible to your kind thought of getting me out of it. I would get out of it like a shot if I could see my way to do so without damaging the show. But I do not at present. The work is exceedingly distasteful to me, and the atmosphere more so. And, after all, it does offer me some pecuniary support, although as yet there has been no performance of the promise. As I insist on performance, and shall do so vehemently—needs must when the devil drives—it is quite possible that I may be 'self-ejecting' before long, the more so that I have made myself objectionable all around by insisting on certain little matters which appeal to Englishmen rather than to Orientals.[84]

It is not known what so irked Pickthall, though his frustrations show the psychological difficulties faced in the relocation from one cultural environment to another. There was an element of ambiguity in an otherwise open-minded and engaging Englishman. For example on his friendships with the *Ittehat ve Terakki* members he would write, "I am at present 'suspect' of my people here [a reference to his circle of friends in Erenköy, where he resided in Istanbul] because of my supposed 'conversion' to the Committee of Union and Progress…as a matter of fact I think the Committee hopeless, but some of the members worthy of a better cause."[85] Mohamed Ali Jauhar himself was not too impressed by the Bureau's performance, though it is not known whether this had anything to do with Pickthall, Ispahani or Kidwai.[86] British Intelligence, presumably with a well-placed mole, observed that "in November 1919 serious disputes over the working of the Bureau took place between Ispahani, who was urged by Kidwai for his own ends, and Pickthall, who was backed by Yakub Hasan and Capt.

Dixon Johnson. Ispahani, as he had supplied most of the funds, wished to act as dictator, which was resented by Pickthall."[87]

Pickthall kept these problems private, and his Friday sermons at the London Muslim House interleaved a spiritual and political message to the congregations:

> ...and many Muslims fought on the side of the Allies, although the historic Muslim Empire was upon the side of Germany. They relied upon the protestations of the British government that the purpose of the Allies was friendly to Islam, and no religious feeling was involved, and no humiliation of the Muslim power in the world was intended. They believed what they were told...they never dreamt that they were taking part in a crusade for the humiliation of Islam. Yet the Prime Minister of England said....'the name of General Allenby [who led Indian troops in the British army into Jerusalem in November 1917] will for ever be renowned as that of the brilliant commander who fought and won the last and most triumphant of the crusades'...the victory of General Allenby was due to Muslims. It could never have been accomplished without Muslim help.
>
> Were those Muslims fighting a crusade against Islam—a crusade for unjust medieval Christendom? What will be their feelings when they learn that the second Holy Places of El Islam was conquered for the Christians by their effort. What will they think when they know that thousands of their Muslim brothers have been massacred in time of peace in order that a portion of the Muslim Empire may be handed over to Greek Christians? You will say that I am talking politics. No, I am talking religion. I am pleading for Allah's kingdom upon earth.[88]

In December 1919 Pickthall was amongst the signatories—together with the Aga Khan, Lord Ampthill and Ameer Ali—to a memorandum to Prime Minister Lloyd George that "urged upon the Government the imperative necessity of a policy towards Turkey that would lead to appeasement of ferment and unrest among Moslems of the world mainly due to apprehension that it is proposed to further dismember the Turkish Empire and completely destroy the free life and political power of the remaining Moslem States."[89]

In his lecture during Ramadan 1920 he called on "the little band of Muslims of pure English birth" to

> remember in their prayers the Muslim Empire....this year none of us can fail to think of the terrible humiliation which threatens the temporal power of Islam, in the person of the honour of their Holy Prophet...we English Muslims have a special need—I might almost call it a responsibility—to keep this Ramadan, for our country, for the last ten years, has dealt unjustly with Islam...[90]

Pickthall's eloquence conveys the anxiety of Muslims of that era. In another talk he was even more outspoken:

> Europe's greatest scoundrels think themselves supreme, and are behaving like a gang of robbers, shamelessly, with no thought of Allah and of their duty towards humanity, with no thought of the Judgement which awaits them. They think themselves the Lords. They are in truth the scum.[91]

Pickthall decided to leave Britain, explaining his position to Aubrey Herbert in another letter in July 1920:

> This is to tell you (what I fear will shock you very much) that I have accepted the editorship of the Bombay Chronicle, an Indian nationalist newspaper. If you want to know the primal reason for my taking such a step, it is simply economic pressure. I cannot afford to live in England, and the offer of a salary of 1400 rupees a month came to me as a positive godsend at the moment of almost of despair....I have not the money sense, any more than the diplomatic. If you can say a word for me anywhere, please do. I am afraid of being boycotted by English people, which means a one-sided view and therefore a false judgement...forgive me if you can for

> going so far from the direction you would chose for me, but believe that I still preserve the straight path of Islam and mean to keep it.[92]

India's gain was to be Britain's loss—particularly for Muslims of Britain who lost a leader around whom the community could have rallied and organised. Muslim philanthropists of the time lacked the vision to ensure that someone of Pickthall's abilities would be free of financial worries.

He continued his contact with the Khilafatists when he moved to India in 1920 as editor of the Bombay Chronicle. As details of the Peace Conferences became known, concern mounted amongst Indian Muslims, particularly as Britain and other 'Great Powers' encouraged a Greek army invasion of Anatolia. The CUP leadership was still held in affection by the masses. When Talaat Pasha was assassinated by an Armenian in Berlin in 1921, over ten thousand people attended a rally in Bombay that was addressed by Pickthall. In his speech, Pickthall notes, "I tried to tell them what a brave man Talaat was, and that sudden death was what he would have always chosen, and how such a death…was really a glorious martyrdom."[93] In July 1922 Pickthall presided over the Sind Khilafat Conference, and backed the alliance of the Ali Brothers with Gandhi:

> I know there are some people who think it wrong for Muslims to accept the leadership of a Hindu. But I think that a Hindu saint who lives upon a higher plane is a better guide for Muslims than a Muslim sinner who lives upon a lower plane, for upon the higher plane there is but one law for Muslims, Hindus, Christians, Jews or any man and that law is the divine law revealed in the Quran-e-Sharif.[94]

The Khilafatist cause was thrown in disarray when Mustafa Kamal's Turkish republic in a fait accompli in March 1924 ordered Abdulmecid Effendi and the entire Ottoman dynasty to leave the country. The Indian Khilafatists planned to send a delegation, including Pickthall, to Turkey so that "people in power in Angora [Ankara] should be convinced of maintaining the Turkish connection with the Khilafa" but the Government of India refused them passports.[95] Faced with Mustafa Kamal's intransigence, Muslim opinion stood divided on where the mantle would now rest with various alternatives mooted, including the Sennousi Shaikh, Ali ibn Hussein and Abdul Aziz ibn Saud. The debate petered out with the realisation that the Muslim world no longer controlled its own destiny in matters of political autonomy.

Relinquishing the editorship of Bombay Chronicle, in 1925 Pickthall became the Principal of the Chadarghat High School for Boys in the principality of Hyderabad, and later adviser to the Nizam. He helped Lord Headley when he visited India on a fund-raising tour for collect funds for a mosque in London—Headley returned with a donation of £60,000 from the Nizam. Pickthall also acted as secretary to the Hyderabad Delegation to the 1930 Round Table Conference on India in London. At the time, the Indian princely states, like the Nizam's, had been assured the right to independence in any future settlement. Pickthall was not to know that this too was another of the Empire's broken promises. His years in Hyderabad were happy and fulfilling—he was also editing the premier English language Islamic journal of the day, 'Islamic Culture', working as an educationalist and mentor, delivering lectures including the series of Madras lectures in 1926 later published as 'The Cultural Side of Islam', and finalising his translation of the Qur'an.

❖

Just as Pickthall chose relocation to India, Philby's *hijrah* was to Arabia in October 1925. No longer on HMG's payroll, he established a commercial venture in Jedda, Sharqieh Ltd. Rumours surfaced in 1927 that he had entered the fold of Islam, but the epiphany came three years later:

> Jidda had been sweltering under a long spell of its foulest weather…I had been working rather hard…and one afternoon, early in August, my head went down on the table like a log and the world seemed to be turning somersaults about me… on recovering from that I confess I felt a bit alarmed, but my mind seemed to be working normally, and I began to consider what I should do in the circumstances. It was then I made my decision….on the afternoon of 7th August 1930, making to my staff the excuse that I had to meet the Finance Minister in Wadi Fatima to discuss some business matters, I got into my Arab garments and drove off in my green Ford car—out of the old life into the new. It happened to be a good day for augury, the birthday of the Prophet Muhammad himself on the twelfth day of Rabi' al Awwal, A.H. 1348…[96]

He chose the name 'Abdullah' for himself.

The revenge he had promised Bullard was to take a commercial form—advising Abdul Aziz ibn Saud to look towards American rather than British collaborations. Economic success gave him a measure of contentment, even marrying an Arab at the suggestion of his benefactor. Philby became a courtier and advisor to the newly declared 'King of the Hejaz' on diverse matters:

> Just about the time of the pilgrimage of April 1931, I was riding in the King's car at Mecca and found his Majesty obviously in the depths of depression. I asked him what the trouble was, and he told me frankly that his Treasury was empty and that he didn't see how his government could make both ends meet in the coming year. It owed about £300,000 in debts of various kinds, its credit was completely exhausted, and its pilgrimage revenues were down by some 75%. The situation was to all appearances desperate and having watched its

development very carefully for some time, I ventured to offer a piece of advice and a piece of criticism. The venture was that the Government should declare a moratorium on all state debts for the time being, and, as I was a substantial creditor, such advice was clearly altruistic. It was accepted and I was privileged to arrange the details of the moratorium with the Minister of Finance…my criticism was couched in more romantic terms. "You", I said to his Majesty, "are like a man fast asleep on top of a gold-mine, complaining of poverty but unwilling to get up and see what he his sleeping on". He asked me to elucidate and I told him that his country was in all probability full of oil and gold and I could not understand his objection to exploiting it if he was in real need. "Well, Philby", he replied, "I assure you that if anyone would hand over me a million pounds now, he could have the concessions for exploiting all that my country possesses…"[97]

Philby's sense of public duty led him to take the initiative on issues relating to the Islamic calendar and moon sightings. Much like Pickthall finding it difficult to adjust to work at the Islamic Information Bureau, Philby did not find the going straight-forward:

For a good many years, when the Nautical Almanac was available a couple of years in advance, I used to supply these calculations [probability of sighting the new moon] …the trouble arises from the fact that the 'bringer of good tidings' is always suitably rewarded: hence the kindness of their eyesight'.[98]

He also pursued his passions in ornithology, archaeology, fossil hunting and desert exploration for which he received a medal from the Royal Geographical Society. His biographer Elizabeth Monroe dwells on his desert treks, capturing Philby's boy-like curiosity even in middle age:

Even when at the end of his tether owing to hunger, thirst or exasperation, Philby was never too tired to take notes and use

> his instruments to determine where they were; his thumbed notebook preserved at the Royal Geographic Society in London, record every change of terrain and shift of direction, each plant observed, each snake or insect seen, each trace of bird or animal…[99]

He had a minor role in the Palestine Conference in London in 1939 as an advisor to Faisal ibn Abdul Aziz, but then began acting as a go-between for a Zionist offer to Abdul Aziz ibn Saud. The reasons this are unclear, particularly given his earlier strictures on the Zionist Herbert Samuel. Perhaps there always remain some less-straightforward aspects in people's characters. This was not the sole example of Philby's ambiguities. He too possessed an enigmatic aspect to his personality at par with Pickthall's Masonic interests. While serving in the Punjab, Philby had run up against the Qadianis after having had to judge in a murder trial in which one of the members of this cult was incriminated. Philby judged against the Qadiani, and was later rebuked for hasty action by his superiors.[100] Philby was fully aware of Mirza Ghulam Ahmad's claim to be a messiah, yet in 1926 he was willing to serve as a go-between in a strange scheme in which the Wahhabi Abdul Aziz Ibn Saud's son, Faisal, would attend the opening of a Qadiani place of worship in South London![101]

Once World War II was declared, Philby found himself in a no-man's land. He blamed the military disaster in France to Britain's failure to take the initiative by invading Belgium and Holland.[102] Such statements were a threat to morale, and en route from Saudi Arabia for a lecture tour in the United States, he was detained in Karachi and put on a steamer to Liverpool and then placed in detention. His faults were the subject of many internal memos between the Colonial Office and other departments:

> His [Philby's] trouble seems to have been unrestrained and sometimes violent attacks on the British Government, on which, recently in Arabia he is said to have habitually heaped scorn and insult. Throughout his life, his manners and conversations are said to have been aggressive and arrogant... while this recent mood persists, he is the type of person who can scarcely fail to do harm to this country's war effort.[103]

These remarks echo some of the officials' sentiments towards Pickthall two decades or so earlier. Disagreement with Government policy rapidly becomes an issue of 'disloyalty' and 'security threats'. Philby, in the words of a very superior Secretary for the Colonies, was "a bit of a *mauvais coucheur.*"[104]

Philby was not detained in prison long, but he emerged undeterred as an advocate of Arab national autonomy, and ever-ready to remind British policy makers of their past deceits. The Special Branch monitored his movements and activities, including a meeting organised by the Islamic Society in June 1945. A report noted that Philby:

> ...strongly attacked British policy in the Middle East and declared that broken promises were not only a feature of French policy. Britain was equally guilty of breach of faith and stood condemned in the Middle East. This country had betrayed the Arab States of Iraq, Palestine and Egypt which today were free only in name. The British military occupation of Egypt and Iraq was inexcusable and as unjust as the French occupation of the Levant States. If France was compelled to withdraw from the Levant then Britain should withdraw her forces from Egypt and Iraq as we had promised those countries complete independence and were bound to honour this pledge.[105]

In 1945 most people had forgotten the Sykes-Picot and McMahon-Hussein pact legacies, but not Philby who remained a reminder of uncomfortable home truths.

Philby's strictures also ranged further afield. He was scathing about American use of atomic weapons against Japan:

> The massacres at Hiroshima and Nagasaki are remembered only as the prelude of final victory in the Second World War; and, so far as I know, no voice, at least no effective voice, has ever been raised in protest against those atrocities, or in condemnation of those responsible for their perpetration. We do not really know who those people were, though legend attributes the credit for the deed to President Truman himself, and it is possible that the final dreadful decision was his. If so, he will presumably have to account for his action before a higher tribunal than any we have on earth: not only for his action then, but for the consequences for the door that has been opened wide to similar and worst crimes in the future....[106]

Perhaps it is little wonder that Abdullah Philby's son, Kim, was to seek revolutionary change to replace the corrupt systems of the day. Kim became enamoured by communist ideals while at Cambridge and was recruited by the KGB.

❖

Pickthall died on 18th May 1936 in Cornwall. The last words he had written the previous night were from the Qur'an: "Whosoever surrendereth his purpose to Allah, while doing good, his reward is with Allah; and there shall no fear come upon them neither shall they grieve."[107]

In Pickthall's reflections on religion one phrase stands out as a leitmotif—'die before you die':

> Obedience to Allah's laws involves a figurative death. *Die before you die*. That is El Islam. Brethren, if we are proper Muslims, we do that every time we say our prayers. When we bow our heads we vow obedience to our Lord in this world, and when we press our foreheads to the ground we die. Can anyone in that position, prostrate before the unseen King of this and every world, count his property, friends, his

> relatives, his pedigree, his grandeur, or his respectability as worth anything at all? He is divested of all chance possessions and accessories. He is naked and alone as in the hour of death, as far as earthly ties are concerned—alone as is the soul of every man and woman from the cradle to the grave.[108]
>
> *Die before you die*! That is the injunction of our lord Muhammad, the man whom Allah led up to the very focus of celestial light. The public worship and the public duties possess no spiritual value until that is done...the public acts demanded of us form a bond of brotherhood between believers of all races and languages—the only bond for a religion which admits no priesthood and no sacraments. But when the act of self-surrender is complete they are much more than that. They are no longer a mere duty; they are a delight...that is the change which Allah brings to pass within the souls of all true Muslims.[109]
>
> The division between this world and the other vanishes for the true Muslim, since Allah is the Lord of the Heavens and the Earth, the Sovereign of this world just as much as the others. The other life has its beginning now, and not at death, for all who perform the act of Al-Islam—that self-Surrender to the will of Allah which the Holy Prophet meant when he advised us: *Die before you die* (*mauthu qabl an tamuthu*).[110]

It is a phrase that conveys Pickthall's depth of faith. It is no wonder that he devoted years of his life to ponder on the Qur'an and work on a translation. Of this effort he would write: "No translation gives the least idea of the beauty and fire of inspiration of that book in Arabic; but no translation can conceal from you the fact that it contains a vision and a law for all humanity."[111]

❖

Philby's biographer Elizabeth Monroe maintained a scepticism about Philby's religious commitment. She also displays her own prejudices: "once he became a Muslim and had access to Ibn Saud's court, he was able to satisfy his sexual appetite in Arabia. The Koran allows men to have intercourse with slaves, and as well as receiving presents of these from time to time, he had access to concubines of princes."[112]

It may be that uninterested in religion herself, she could not tune-in to the spiritual side of her subject's personality. There may well have been an ebb and flow in Abdullah Philby's religious commitment, but that is part of the human condition. Philby's own words and writings do not reflect the mercenary attitude suggested by Monroe.

The preface to his book 'Forty Years in the Wilderness', published in 1957, three years prior to his death, was dedicated to his mother, with the front piece quoting from the Qur'an: "Thy Lord hath decreed that ye worship none but Him and that ye be kind to parents... And lower unto them the wing of submission through mercy, and say: My Lord! Have mercy on them both as they did care for me when I was little."

In a reflection in the same work, Philby noted:

> ...throughout the years that have followed I have never posed as a professor of Muslim theology: preferring the humbler role of a *Talib 'Ilm*, a searcher after knowledge. Islam is an authoritarian creed, based firmly on God's word as conveyed to humanity in the Qur'an, and on the precepts and practices of the Prophet; and I have always accepted as authoritative and binding the interpretation of all that falls within those limits by the learned men, the *Ulama*, who have spent their lives in the study and elucidation thereof...it is in Arabia and Islam that I have found in actual being an easy social system well adjusted to the needs of humanity, until man was tempted by all the apparatus of western materialism to wander among the 'roses and raptures' of exotic gardens.[113]

There is no doubting his feeling of solidarity with Muslims. While based in Jedda, he was of assistance to English hajjis from Britain, most notably to Lady Evelyn Zainab Cobbold. His periods of stay in Britain were much occupied with speaking engagements and invitations.[114] He attended the opening of the East London Mosque on Commercial Road in August 1941 and its trustees soon after sought his help in running the attached Islamic Cultural Centre.[115] Lady Buchanan Smith, President of the Muslim Society in Great Britain invited him to speak at its event to mark the Prophet's Birthday in March 1942 and in December the same year he spoke on Id ul Adha at the East London Mosque on brotherhood and democracy.[116] In December 1943 he led the Eid prayers and delivered the khuṭbah at the Shah Jehan Mosque, at the invitation of Maulvi Abdul Majid of the Woking Muslim Mission and Literary Trust. Philby also spoke at Caxton Hall in Victoria, a public meeting hall frequently used by Muslim organisations of the period. For example it was the venue of his talk 'The Significance of the Prophet's Mission' organised by the Muslim Society in Great Britain in March 1945. Once the Islamic Cultural Centre near Regent's Park was inaugurated that year, he was invited on several occasions as a speaker, lecturing on themes such as 'Arab Culture from Earliest Times' in June 1948.

Philby, unlike Pickthall, did not choose retirement in England, and died in Beirut in 1960.

In concluding one of his speeches to a Muslim audience in 1942, he conveyed sentiments that would have been very much Pickthall's as well:

> … I would just like to say a few words about the basic idea of Islam. The word is generally understood as signifying 'peace' or 'resignation to the will of God'. In my opinion, however, if I may venture to express it in the presence of many better qualified to express an opinion than I am, those meanings are secondary or derivative meanings of the word. After all the

> word is, as you all know, an Arabic word derived from the root SLM, the basic idea of which seems to me to be safety or salvation ….in the strictest ecclesiastical sense salvation from hell-fire but in general salvation from danger or misfortune. And you must remember that in the strictest Muslim sense such salvation depends entirely on the will of God.[117]

He too considered translating the Qur'an, but a publisher deal fell through.

Analyses

As the balance of military power tilted away from Ottoman Turkey during the Great War, Pickthall was worried, "this is an anxious time for all of us. We do not know what will happen next."[118] Philby's assessments belong to a later period when oil wealth on a scale unimaginable was transforming the Middle East. Pickthall was alert to the military disarmament of the Muslim world; Philby to the cultural disarmament that would follow. Both had ideas on the Muslim world's strengths and problems and opportunities for the future. Both urged Muslims to retain their fellowship of the *ummah* and a capacity for resistance.

In 1919, after the defeat of Ottoman Turkey, Pickthall observed in a speech in England:

> …it is with a thrill of pride that I see Sunni and Shi'a standing side by side as brothers in firm demand for what is just and right…. Muslims, [they] are representatives of an ideal more advanced than any that prevails in Europe. If they forsake that high ideal of brotherhood for the lower one of national pride, they (in the words of the Qur'an) 'barter the higher for the lower'…whatever nationalism has appeared in Muslim countries has been purely imitative and artificial, the work of foreign influences, foreign money. I speak of nationalism in the European sense. Pan-Islamism—which is true Islamic

> patriotism ...would of course, if left alone, be a useful and progressive movement, aiming at the raising of Muslim brotherhood in every land by education. A nationalistic movement, on the other hand is an aggressive movement, jealous of all other nationalities and heedless of religion. There is nothing that we Muslims ought to guard more jealously than the brotherhood of believers.[119]

Pickthall concluded the speech with a plea for intra-Muslim tolerance:

> I dare say that some of you English Muslims are occasionally impatient at some of the customs of the Muslim world, at some of the minute details of religious practice which our Oriental brethren think of very great importance. Well, if you have in you the true Islamic spirit, you will be careful of those little matters for your brother's sake, who loves them. They may be little in themselves. A nail or a rivet is a small thing. And these small things hold us all together.[120]

Given the times, it is interesting that Pickthall did not shrink from deploying a military simile:

> The whole of the institutions of Islam are designed...to produce in the first place righteous men and women and in the second place to bind them together in brotherhood as compact and well-disciplined as an army which may at any moment have to be mobilised.[121]

Pickthall's eloquent Eid Khuṭbah in June 1919 similarly called on the congregation to delve into their Islamic values to withstand the external onslaughts such as the humiliating peace terms being imposed on the defeated:

> Seek Him; you will surely find Him. Strive in His way, be constant and sincere in prayer, be kind and charitable and you will be conscious of His active help; you will know true happiness in the consciousness of Allah's Kingdom upon earth. Do all that is in your power to spread true knowledge of

> Islam among our English people, dispelling the false notions and prejudices which still prevail among so many English Christians. Make your Islam respected and beloved in your own circles and give the lie to those who say false things about the Faith. And if, in the course of your striving, you should meet persecution, do not fear it. It is good that "there should come to you the like to that which came to those who passed before you". Then you will know that Allah's help is coming to you. "Now truly Allah's help is very nigh."[122]

When in 1926 Pickthall was invited by the Muslim community in Madras to give a series of lectures he placed much emphasis on the pursuit of knowledge and education. He declared that "neither the Holy Qur'an nor the Holy Prophet ever contemplated the existence of an ignorant Muslim. Indeed ignorant Muslim is a contradiction in terms."[123] He was highly critical of the scholastic trend in religious scholarship:

> the ulema who sought knowledge 'even though it were in China' were no more. In their place stood men bearing the same high name of ulema, claiming the same reverence, but who sought knowledge only in a limited area, the area of Islam as they conceived it…a growth of pride accompanied the cult of ignorance.[124]

His poor opinion of the *'ulamā'* proved to be a self-fulfilling prophecy: when he visited Al-Azhar a few years later to seek their advice on his English translation of the Qur'an, he met petty and ill-informed criticism. Pickthall also held that "true Sufism is the spirit as against blind worship of the letter of Islam and the true Sufis have kept the spirit alive and pure through days when the majority of Muslims saw the letter only."[125]

In the Madras lectures Pickthall also raised his concerns at trends to marginalise the Islamic code in day-to-day life. He could foresee the importance of the *maqāṣid al-Sharī'ah*:

> We all agree that it is desirable that the truths of Islam should

> be made known and, as far as possible, commended to the modern world. But some among us seem to think that the way so to commend them is to disregard the Shariah as something antiquated; and to present Islam as a religion without a Law—a mere matter of personal belief, of abstract thought and of detached opinion…
>
> If the Muslims have declined through their neglect of certain portions of the Shariah, that is no reason for discarding the remaining portions, but rather for restoring the whole and observing it with more intelligence.
>
> We want a clear code of the main principles and injunctions which can be placed in the hands of every Muslim, every Muslimah. At present, in existing works on Fiqh, we are confronted with the manifest absurdity that personal matters like the position in which the believers stand to pray, are made of equal importance with first principles, like that law forbidding murder.
>
> We have to distinguish once for all between that which is essential and of permanent homage value and that which was the currency of a particular historical period.[126]

Pickthall also extended the discussion to Islamic economics:

> …the Muslim system of finance was a complete system. Only it is difficult for modern men of affairs even to begin to understand it, because its aim was not private profit or state profit, but public profit, the welfare and progress of the whole Muslim brotherhood. It was a potent factor in the success of the Muslim civilisation, and the decline of that civilisation synchronised with the gradual neglect of it…it seems to me essential that Muslims of today should study carefully the proper Islamic system of finance.[127]

Pickthall's conception of Islam as a complete way of life anticipated the formulation of the Islamic movements that were to emerge a decade later. He was drawn to the ideas of his old acquaintance S'aid Halim Pasha, though at the time of their meeting their mutual impressions were rather reserved.[128] The

Madras lectures contain several references to Halim Pasha's "remarkable work in Turkish, 'Islamlashmaq', an essay which aims to depict the true Islamic state in modern times and contrast it with existing forms of government."[129]

In his eighth lecture in the Madras series of 1926, entitled 'The City of Islam', Pickthall provided the audience with an outline of 'Islamlashmaq', evidently reflecting a personal endorsement:

> The principle points of Prince S'aid Halim's presentment of the modern Islamic State may be thus summarised. The distinction between secular and religious in matters of administration, education, policy and general dealing has no right whatever to exist in the Islamic State. Where Allah is King the secular becomes religious. All that would remain would be persons specially learned in matters of religion, the reverence paid to whom would be entirely owing to their knowledge as displayed in actual work, from among their number the members of the Legislative body would be elected by the people's representatives. In short, the first thing to be done is to get rid altogether of that 'pseudo-priesthood' to which S'aid Halim refers as the Chief Misleader of the Muslim World.
>
> The State itself having been 'Islamised' and organised upon the lines I have already indicated and having the advice of experts in Islamic ethics, politics and sociology, who alone possess the right (due to their competence) to frame new laws, will proceed on lines consistent with the basic principles of the Shariah such as:
> equality of all individuals, male and female, before the law;
> universal education both of males and females;
> absolute religious tolerance;
> prohibition of usury...;
> prohibition of the sale of alcoholic drink;
> prohibition of gambling;
> the institutions of zakat and Beyt-ul-Mal…;

> respect for the rights of property within the limits laid down by the sacred law;
> the sanctity of all contracts;
> the institution of marriage as a civil contract between free individuals…; the maintenance of a decent reserve between the sexes, for the safety of women;
> the Islamic law of inheritance…;
> respect for women's personal, property and rights;
> respect for the rights of children….;
> universal military training as distinct from conscription;
> the Islamic regulations concerning foreign policy; sanctity of treaties, prohibition of aggressive nationalism and welfare; strict observance of the Islamic laws of war….
> I think that this is what may be truly described as an 'advanced' programme for any modern state.[130]

Pickthall added, "Islam offers a complete political and social system as an alternative to socialism, fascism, syndicalism, bolshevism and all other 'isms' offered as an alternative."[131]

Pickthall's audience in Madras were thus provided ideas on the possibilities of reconstituting the Islamic sovereign state in an age without an Ottoman Caliphate. The Indian Muslim literary and intellectual world of the period was remarkably well-informed, with an arc of talent spanning Lahore-Delhi-Hyderabad. Pickthall's ideas would have inspired other Muslim activists of the period to retain the vision of an Islamic polity and Islamic state. Iqbal for example was to refer to S'aid Halim Pashi both in his famous Madras lectures of 1929 but also in *Javid Nama* published in 1932.[132]

Pickthall's ideas represented a transition from the notion of a single all-powerful point of authority—the Caliph—to councils of experts. He was sceptical of mass electoral politics: "Islam has no belief in the collective infallibility of those who are individually incompetent, and it has no faith in the majority of the ignorant."[133] It was an elitist vision which was not to sit comfortably with people's expectations later in the twentieth century.

For Pickthall, it was the destiny of believers to create a "Kingdom of Allah" on earth—a theme found not only in his earlier writings and speeches such as his Eid Khuṭbah of 1919 but in the third and fifth of his Madras lectures. Given the interchange of ideas of the period, it is not surprising to see its expression as well in the notion of *'hukumat-ilahyia'* in the religious literature of the day. This was a term to be central for Maulana Maudoodi, who in the 1925-28 period, though only in his twenties, had established himself as a leading campaigning journalist in the Urdu religious press.

❖

Philby also grappled with the implications of the loss of a Muslim centre of power following Ottoman Turkey's defeat in World War I. He lacked Pickthall's concrete way of thinking, but there was a shared idealism. Writing in 1938 he noted:

> ...all parties would probably agree that Caliphate ceased to be anything more than an empty name when the greatest of the Islamic states ceased to count as a Great Power—when Islam, in other words, ceased to mistress of her own destiny in a world effectively controlled by Christendom...[Islam] has no illusions on the subject. It does not regard the Prophet's mantle as a decoration to be conferred on some deserving prince, but as a standard to be carried, always at the post of danger, by a warrior willing and competent to lead a crescentade against the growing supremacy of Christendom, against the increasing encroachment on what remains of Islamic independence and freedom. An Abyssinian eunuch and slaves have been caliphs before—an Abyssinian eunuch capable, for instance of ridding Palestine of its Jewish and British usurpers would have a better title to the Caliphate in

> the eyes of Islam than any of the crowned heads today, forced by their military weakness to acquiesce mutely in a situation that Islam regards as a scandal. Islam expects its Caliph to do their duty, and no prince, however great, can expect its acclamations until he has shown his worth in defence of its long neglected rights.....[134]

Much like Pickthall, Philby believed that Islam's strength rested on its unique sense of fellowship that could transcend race and class. He wrote out in long-hand the speech he had been invited to deliver by the Muslim Society of Great Britain on the occasion of the Prophet's Birthday—on letterhead of the Athenaeum Club where he was staying in 1942 during some of the World War II years—reflecting on this aspect of Islam:

> ...in Arabia today and at Mecca, the very birthplace of Islam and its Prophet, there is still something of the unity and brotherhood of Islam, which the Prophet himself bequeathed to his followers in the last year of his life....[135]

Philby's speech included an assessment of the contemporary Muslim world, his concern for its autonomy and independence, warnings and a message of hope:

> ...when you come to think of it the world into which the Prophet Muhammad was born and in which he lived bears a remarkable resemblance to our world of today. It was a world of war and rumours of war. It was a world in which two great Empires were in conflict with each other: in which two very different ideologies were striving for mastery, sometimes under the conditions of uneasy peace and other times in actual battle. And to pursue the parallel still further, Arabia, though almost surrounded by warring nations, held aloof from the actual conflict, watching the two great giants locked in strife and totally unaware of the destiny which awaited her in due course...
>
> Many times he [the Prophet] must have pondered during his long wanderings in the mountains of Mecca tending to his

sheep and later during his caravan journeys to Damascus and other places on the fringe of the Roman Empire—many times he must have pondered how military might alone is not the final arbiter of human destinies and how virtue and right may triumph over evil if it be the will of God…

It is important for you to realise that all the independent States of Islam today are maintaining an attitude of neutrality towards the war—Turkey, Egypt, Iraq, Persia, Afghanistan, Saudi Arabia and the Yaman. Other Islamic countries like Syria, Palestine, Trans-Jordan, the Sudan and the Persian Gulf principalities are involved in the war as vassals of the Great Powers. And many Muslim soldiers, as you know, are fighting bravely by the side of soldiers of other religions in this war as subjects of the Great Powers—Great Britain, France, Italy and Russia. And many millions of Muslims have recently passed, as a result of the war, under the domination of Japan. In a word, the position of Islam is not a very happy one.

Islam is surrounded by grave dangers. It almost seems as if Islam were surrounded by the disagreeable alternatives of remaining, for the most part, under the domination of one group of Great Powers or passing under the domination of another group. And it may be stated as a fact that neither of these alternatives being attractive, the main aim of all the Islamic communities of the world is to achieve effectively the status of real independence…that I think you will agree is the aim of Islam as a whole. And if you will go back in your thoughts to the time of the Prophet and particularly to that last pilgrimage of the tenth year of the Hijra, when he realised that the days of his mission were drawing to a close for he had only three months of life left to him at the time and he had a presentiment that the end was near, you will understand that his last public act, his last service to his people was the promulgation of an Islamic Charter—a charter of freedom for all time to come under the blessing of God. He had actually sent out the first of the great Muslim armies which were destined to vindicate that freedom against the two strongest Powers of the world, but he was not spared to see the astonishing results they achieved...

In our time we have seen the decline and fall of the once great Turkish Empire, and with its fall many may have felt that Islam as a political force in the world was dead. Yet it was not so. Out of the ashes of the Turkish Empire arose a new spirit in Islam, manifested in the rise of a number of new Islamic States and the rejuvenation of old ones…perhaps we can include the Islamic State of India, known as Pakistan—stand forth as young but vigorous nations of whose future one need not despair.

None of them can be regarded as potential Great Powers, but with 250 millions of Muslims in the world there is no reason to suppose that someday a Great Power will not arise out of them to give Islam as a whole its proper place in the political and social counsels of the world. But the first thing necessary is that Islam should concentrate on the difficult task of achieving unity of purpose, as it in fact concentrates on its unswerving belief in the unity of God. With unity Islam has nothing to fear, but the Prophet, whose birthday we celebrate today, warned Islam of the dangers of dispersion and its consequences. 'This people', he declared, 'will be split into seventy-three factions and all of them are destined for the fire except one, all that walk in the way I walk in and my companions'.

That to my mind is always the supreme factor, the supreme lesson of Islam—the paramount necessity of unity as a source of strength….to those of you here who are not Muslims I would say this, I would say that it is absolutely contrary to the principles and precepts of Islam that any Muslim should want to live under foreign rule. I would ask you therefore to realise the simple fact that every Islamic community or state desires independence and is still far from convinced that its independence is included in the war-aims of any of the warring Powers. At the same time I would say to the Muslims here, and indeed to Muslims all over the world, that unless they can achieve unity amongst themselves they will neither be worthy of such independence nor able to use

> such independence for the benefit of Islam or the world in general.
>
> I am convinced that a great future awaits Islam in the new world, which will come into being after this war and which will be very different from the bad old world which we have now almost forgotten. But everything depends on the efforts we ourselves make to create such a new world. We must not forget that during the last world war we were freely promised that everything would be changed for the better after it. But we now know that those promises were never realised. During the last twenty years there has been nothing but discontent and restlessness and frustration, worse than anything the world has ever known since the dark ages. And it has all ended in another catastrophe more frightful than the last. And it can truly be said that 'the last state of the world has become worse than the first'. So it is our business to see that sort of set-back doesn't happen again when the present period of tribulation is ended. And Islam, if it is true to the principles and precepts of its Prophet, has a great part to play in bringing the world back to sanity some day.

Philby concluded his address reverting to some of the values of Muslim society that had first enchanted him twenty years earlier. In his analysis the world must

> to a great extent turn away from the material implications of western (so-called) civilisation and go back to something like the old codes of morality and humanity which, as we are inclined to forget, came to us originally from 'the wise men of the East'. In the East they are still observed to a considerable extent in spite of the corrupting influences of the west. We people of the West are rather inclined to regard the peoples of the East as simple-minded and primitive folk because they take their religion seriously. But that is surely very far from being the case, and the West has a great deal to learn from countries like Arabia in the matter of reconciling the activities of our daily life with the requirements of the moral codes

we profess to follow. Islam at any rate uncompromisingly demands adherence to its moral code in spite of any inconvenience it may entail. At the same time its code is based on recognition of the frailty of human nature and none of its demands are excessive. That is probably due to the fact that, although divinely inspired, the Prophet Muhammad himself never claimed to be anything but a human being like the rest of mankind. 'Ana bashrun mithlukum' he declared. 'I am a human being like yourselves.

On that note I will close. We celebrate today the birth of one of the greatest men in all history. He left a message which has made a great appeal to a very large section of humanity through the ages. And the burden, the outstanding motif, of that message is Glory to God in the highest, and on earth peace, goodwill toward men—Peace through Salvation. And when I say that I would ask you to realise that the Prophet Muhammad was not a Pacifist. As I have told you almost his last act was to send out an army to fight for peace and freedom.

In an article in the Evening Standard a year later, Philby boldly reiterated his stand on the contemporary need for Islam's values:

> The logic of Islam is unassailable, and it is the only way of life yet propounded which has attempted—with no mean measure of success—to apply the basic principles of democracy to human society. Islam has largely succeeded where Britain, America and France have failed, despite all their great charters of liberty, equality and fraternity. Let us beware of all efforts to extinguish the shining light of its independence or cover it with the bushel of a mechanised civilisation.[136]

The independence which Philby dreamt about did come about, but in a space of five decades, the federation-style Ottoman dispensation was replaced by national rivalries and repressive regimes that were client states of a new imperial power.

Philby returned to Saudi Arabia after World War II, but characteristically he could not hold his peace on the excesses and corruption of the royal princes after Abdul Aziz ibn Saud—"the wartime bounty of Britain and America and the subsequent flood of oil shattered all restraints on human rapacity."[137]

The new symbols of prosperity had penetrated beyond the palaces:

> I was profoundly shocked…when one of the chiefs of the Qahtan, the premier tribe of Southern Arabia with a pedigree going back to the Jocktan of Genesis, told me with genuine pride and satisfaction that his two elder sons were doing very well: as chauffeurs in the service of the Arabian American Oil Company, earning a salary of £20 a month![138]

He saw a historical parallel in the way the country was becoming dependent on foreign expertise and foreign benefactors: "the old story of 'capitulations' seems to be in process of repetition in a slightly different context: *plus ça change, plus c'est la meme chose!*"[139]

❖

One of Pickthall's friends remarked about him on his death, "no one could be a stricter conserver of the foregrounds of his own will, and of the ultimate secrets of his personality."[140] The same applies to some extent to Abdullah Philby as well. It is the rare biographer who can do justice to the full range of his subjects' experiences and motivations. Pickthall and Philby were true friends of the Muslim world, and men of honour and chivalry. Theirs were voices of conscience, outspoken in criticisms of their own government, and of Muslim conduct when it fell short of the mark. Pickthall, in this description of the Prophet, peace be on him, may have been subconsciously reflecting his own aspiration: "our Prophet was a gentle and forbearing man, averse to passionate excess of every kind."[141] For neither man the ideology 'My Country, right or wrong' was paramount.

Being English, they had been conditioned in a self-belief of a nation founded on decency and fair play. Unlike many others, they belonged to an elite circle that knew full well their Government's pledges and solemn undertakings. When these were not honoured, their inner voice would not allow them to remain silent.

Their lives straddled a painful period of Muslim history when military disarmament was followed by cultural disarmament—the door of *jihād* was obstructed and so too of *ijtihād*. They resisted this trend and so their memories are important for us today. We ought to dwell awhile at the intersection of individuals' lives and momentous historical movements, and reflect. We need to retain their boldness and capacity to imagine alternative futures.

Notes

1. Peter Clark, 'Marmaduke Pickthall, British Muslim', Quartet Books, 1986; for Clark's criticisms of Pickthall's attitude towards Armenians see pp. 33-34.
2. Abdal Hakim Murad, 'Marmaduke Pickthall, A Brief Biography', Seasons—Summer 2004.
3. Lawrence M Stratton, 'Tory Muslim: The conversion of Marmaduke Pickthall', Koinonia, XVI, 2004.
4. Elizabeth Monroe, 'Philby of Arabia', Quartet Books, 1980.
5. See William Facey, 'From Mayfair to Mecca', in 'Lady Evelyn Cobbold, Pilgrimage to Mecca', Arabian Publishing, 2008.
6. Ibid. p. 61.

7. See 'Loneliness—a Study of the Human Condition', Hutchinson, 1966; she also has passing references to Pickthall in 'Rebel's Ride', Hutchinson, 1964.
8. Anne Freemantle, 'Loyal Enemy', Hutchinson, 1938; p. 264.
9. H. St John Philby, 'Forty Years in the Wilderness', Robert Hale, 1957; pp. 85-86.
10. M Pickthall, Oriental Encounters, 1918; Introduction [accessible on Google Books].
11. Ibid.
12. Ibid.
13. Abdal Hakim Murad, Op.cit; p. 24.
14. Muhammad Haneef Shahid, 'Writings of Muhammad Marmaduke William Pickthall', Ashraf, Pakistan, 2003; p. 241, citing Islamic Review, May 1919, Vol. 7, No 5, pp. 175-182.
15. Ibid. p. 3.
16. M. Pickthall, Saïd the Fisherman, Methuen, 1903; p. 115.
17. M. Pickthall, With the Turk in Wartime, Dent, 1914 [accessible on http://openlibrary.org/books/OL7208812M/With_the_Turk_in_wartime].
18. Ibid. p. 35.
19. Haneef Shahid, Op.cit; p. 292; Pickthall's letters to his wife Muriel in 1913 were published in Islamic Culture, Hyderabad, Vol. 11, No. 4, October 1937; pp. 419-32.
20. Ibid. p. 289.
21. The Western powers provided no succour to Ottoman Turkey in this period, Britain repeatedly turning down proposals for an Anglo-Turkish alliance—see Feroz Ahmed, 'From Empire to Republic—Essays on the late Ottoman Empire and Modern Turkey', Vol. 1, Istanbul Bilgi University Press, 2008; p. 167.
22. Pickthall, The Turk in Wartime, Op.cit. p. 103.
23. M. Pickthall, 'Cultural Side of Islam', a compilation of lectures first published in 1927; in 'The City of Islam', he notes, "Prince S'aid Halim, whom I knew very well, was a man with practical experience of statesmanship in troubled times…" He was a prince by virtue of being the grandson of Mehmed Ali Pasha, Governor and later Khedive of Egypt.
24. Haneef Shahid, Op.cit; p. ix.
25. Ibid. p. 280. See also Professor Wasti's 'Halil Halid: Anti-imperialist Muslim Intellectual', Middle Eastern Studies, Vol. 29, No. 3, July 1993, pp. 559-579, and 'The Indian Sojourn of Abdulhak

Hamid', Vol. 34, No. 4, October 1999, pp. 33-34 of the same journal. A common friend of both Pickthall and Halil Halid was E.G. Browne at Cambridge, who coincidentally was later to be one of Philby's teachers at Trinity College. AbdulHak Hamid and Halil Halid were pro-Consuls at the Ottoman Embassy in London, serving at different times.

26. Freemantle, Op.cit; p. 258; Pickthall's friend Refaat Bey was also a Mason, and according to Ottoman historian Ahmet Uçar also a Pan-Islamist (conversation with author, September 2010).

27. Abdullah Quilliam (1856-1932) was also a Mason—see Professor Ron Geaves' 'Islam in Victorian Britain—the life and times of Abdullah Quilliam', Kube Publishing, Markfield, 2010; pp. 108-109. Quilliam was a loyal supporter of Sultan Abdul Hamid II, while Pickthall's network comprised the opposing CUP members—so there may be no need to read any sinister motives in their Masonic associations. Professor Geaves believes that Quilliam assumed the identity of Henri de Leon in later life. When Pickthall became editor of the Islamic Culture, Hyderabad, articles by de Leon appeared in the journal.

28. Philby, 'Arabian Days', Hale, 1948; p. 43.

29. Ibid; p. 278.

30. Ibid; p. 279.

31. Philby, Forty Years, Op.cit. p. 52.

32. Monroe, Op.cit. p. 74.

33. Philby, Arabian Days; Op.cit. p. 279.

34. Philby, Forty Years; Op.cit. p. 39.

35. Op.cit, Saïd the Fisherman; Pickthall referred to a real-life event in 1860—for details see 'Bughyat-ul Talib' by Ibrahim Al-Kayali, Darul Kutub al Islamiya, Beiruth, 2004; pp. 13-14.

36. Philby, 'Arabia of the Wahhabis', Cass 1977 (first edition 1928); p. 323.

37. Philby, Arabian Days, Op.cit; p. 279.

38. The incident occurred in May 1906 and is well described in Elizabeth Longford's biography of Wilfred Scawen Blunt—' A Pilgrimage of Passion', Weidenfeld and Nicolson, 1979; p. 359-360.

39. Clark, Op.cit. p. 16.

40. Monroe, Op.cit. p. 22.

41. Clark, Op.cit. p. 86.

42. Feroz Ahmad, From Empire to Republic, Vol. 1, Istanbul Bilgi University Press 2008; p. 143, citing Grey to Lowther, 31 July, 1908, FO 800/78.

43. Ibid; p. 18; the legal right was stipulated in the 1878 Treaty of Berlin that ended the Russo-Turkish war and gave Austria the right only to administer Bosnia and Herzegovina. Wilfred Scawen Blunt blamed Edward VII for Britain's acquiescence to this violation. Blunt notes in his Diaries: "His (Edward's) only notable failure was in the affair of Bosnia, and people in England knew little of the conditions to understand how great a failure it was." Blunt, 'My Diaries', v2 1900-1914, Martin Secker; 1920; p. 321.

44. See for example his 'Oriental Encounters' (1918) that draws on his experiences in the Levant in 1894-96. Chapter II, 'A mountain garrison', describes a jealous Armenian; similarly 'As others see us' (1922) depicts scenes of Armenian brigands burning Muslim villages; p. 80.

45. Pickthall, 'Massacres and the Turks: The Other Side", Foreign Affairs, Special Supplement II, 1920; pp.xiv-xvi. An excellent account of this period can also be found in Kamal Beydilli's 'From Küçük Kaynarca to the Collapse', in 'The History of the Ottoman State, Society and Civilisation', ed. E. Ihsanoğlu, IRCICA, Istanbul 2002; pp. 114-121. This includes an account of the Armenian terrorist attempt to assassinate Sultan Abdul Hamid II in 1905.

46. Feroz Ahmed (Op.cit.) notes, "Non-Muslim communities [also] enjoyed extensive privileges under the *millet* system …as the empire declined, the Great Powers began to adopt the millets as clients, exploiting them to further their own interests in the empire…non-Muslims began adopting what amounted to foreign citizenship"; p. 94-95. Pickthall himself was to observe in a speech at the London Muslim House some years later: "the very proofs of our [Muslim] religious tolerance, those Christian subjects whose faith and nationality were safe with us, have been turned against us and are quoted as proof that we were 'unable to assimilate alien elements of population'. Christian Europe has assimilated such elements of population by massacre, by enforced conversion and the stake. We gave them liberty of conscience and self-government"—see Haneef Shahid, Op.cit. p. 30, which cites the Islamic Review, July 1918.

The bogey of Turkish treatment of non-Muslims continues to this day, and this headline is typical: "Council of Europe urges Turkey to respect non-Muslims"—The Tablet, 27th March 2010.

47. Haneef Shahid, Op.cit. p. 280.
48. Ibid. p. 292.
49. Ian Duffield, 'Dusé Mohamed Ali, Afro-Asian solidarity and Pan-Africanism in early twentieth-century London', in 'Essays on the history of Blacks in Britain: From Roman times to the mid-Twentieth Century', ed. Jagdish S. Gundara and Ian Duffield, Aldershot: Avebury, 1992.
50. Clark, Op.cit; p. 20, citing Pickthall's article in New Age, 7 November 1912, XII, p. 8.
51. Duffield, Op.cit.
52. H.F.V. Winstone, 'The Illicit Adventure—the Story of Political and Military Intelligence in the Middle East from 1898 to 1926', Jonathan Cape, 1982; p. 310; Winstone cites FO 371/3062 but the author has not been able to find reference to Pickthall in this file at the Public Record Office, Kew.
53. Clark, Op.cit; p. 31.
54. Jonathan Schneer, 'The Balfour Declaration—the Origins of the Arab-Israeli Conflict', Bloomsbury, 2010; p. 249.
55. Ibid. p. 251.
56. Ibid. p. 252.
57. Pickthall's friend Aubrey Herbert was similarly verbally abused. Herbert wished to write directly to Talaat Pasha, the Ottoman Minister of Interior to negotiate prisoners of war. In July 1917 he sent his draft letter to the Foreign Office, which included the statement, "...in our warfare with the Turkey we have learnt to admire the Turk as a clean fighter and a gallant soldier. I should be very sorry if events subsequent to the battlefield ever changed the feeling of liking and respect which are, I think, mutual between us...." The Foreign Office records have this note in response: "...the 'clean fighting' Turk legend should not be perpetuated and I don't think any Englishman should talk about liking and respect to Talaat, who if we could catch him should be tried and hanged for his Armenian massacres". PRO FO 371/3060.
58. The Central Islamic Society Series—3, 'Muslim Interests in Palestine', Central Islamic Society, London (not dated, but likely 1917).
59. Ibid; p. 10.
60. PRO CAB 24/144, Eastern Report No. 31; August 29, 1917.
61. Haneef Shahid, Op.cit. p.x, footnote 6.
62. Ibid. p. 29.

63. PRO CAB/24/83.
64. In his 'Arabia of the Wahhabis', Philby provides eye-witness accounts of the task. Many of the Nejdi Bedouin harnessed by Abdul Aziz ibn Saud—the Ikhwan—were not entirely stupid and could see the game: "there was clearly some uneasiness in the minds of the Ikhwan lest this project of a campaign against the Shammar, Wahhabis like themselves, might be but the outcome of traffic with the infidel and designed to serve some recondite political aim with which they had no sympathy." Abdul Aziz's political genius lay in his ability to win over this dissent: "Look ye, you people are my army in that I have no army but my God and you. In the days of your ignorance, when you were but robbers and brigands, you were my army and, now that you have taken to the faith and settled in villages, you are still the army on which I rely…if only I would make myself master of the Shammar capital the English would leave all the desert tribes to my rule." Philby continues, "The Wahhabi monarch then unfolded his plans for a sustained attack against Ibn Rashid and, having thus laid his cards on the table, invited the high priest of Washm—no other than Muhammad Ibn Abdul Wahab, brother of Shaikh Abdullah—and other ulama present to declare their opinions as to who was the real enemy of the moment. With one voice they assured the assembled multitude that no other than Ibn Rashid was the arch-enemy, and the Ikhwan, as they do when under the stress of strong emotion, fell to weeping and declaring through their tears that, if only they had been taken into their sovereign's confidence earlier, theywould have come forward to a man without any foreboding"; Op.cit. 'Arabia of the Wahhabis', pp. 102-103.
65. An example of the way Lawrence collated information is provided in this assessment he made of Sherif Hussein of Hejaz and his sons in December 1917 (though it may include his own wishful interpolations): "…the Sheriff is ostensibly a Shafei; in this connection he took up a middle position between moderate Shia and Sunni: it is generally believed that his real beliefs are Zaidi. Sidi Abdulla is definitely a Shia of the Jaaferi wing; Sidi Ali is a Sunni, and a fairly definite one; Sidi Faisal is not a formalist and tends to an undefined undogmatic position, more Shia perhaps than Sunni, but vague. They are all nervous of betraying their real attitudes even to their friends, and maintain a non-committal Shafei profession in public….his [Sherif Hussein's] motives in rebelling against the Turks were two: first is a political object, the liberation of the Arab

world from Turkish domination: this he will effect without question of creed—Christian, Druze, Sunni and Shia meet on a common base of nationality…his second motive was a religious one, purely Islamic in character: it is to provide for the Muhammadan world an independent sovereign, ruling in the Holy Places, of the Sheriff family, whose claims to the spiritual leadership of Islam will be so transcendent as to be generally admitted, but whose weakness in material resources (money, ships and guns) will at once make him acceptable to the Christian Powers and purge Islam of the lunatic idea that it is a polity...”; PRO FO 371/3062.
66. Philby, Arabia of the Wahhabis, Op.cit; p. 332-333.
67. Monroe, Op.cit; p. 109.
68. Ibid. p. 110.
69. Philby, Forty Years in the Wilderness; Op.cit. p. 86; pp. 107-108.
70. Monroe, Op.cit. p. 131.
71. Philby, Arabian Days, Op.cit. pp. 235-236.
72. Monroe, Op.cit. . p. 132.
73. Philby, Forty Years in the Wildnerness, Op.cit. pp. 133-134.
74. Abdul Aziz ibn Saud to King Ali of Hejaz, 17th November 1924: “I regard you personally with the greatest respect, but it was your father’s treatment of the people of the Nejd and other Muslims which caused me to decide on this course of action which I have adopted. If then you are desirous of peace and the avoidance of bloodshed, depart from the Hejaz, and await the decision of the Muslim world. If it chooses you or anyone else, we will accept its decision with the utmost joy. But, if you remain in Hejaz, the responsibility for what may happen will rest on other shoulders than mine [signed—Sultan of Nejd, Abdul Aziz]”; ibid.
75. Philby’s articles on the Hejaz were published in the Daily Telegraph, 13th-18th February 1925. Interestingly, they were picked up by the sharp-eyed twenty-two year old editor of *Jamiat*, the news paper of the Jamiat ul-Ulema in Delhi, Abul ‘Ala Maudoodi—who referred to Philby in an article published on 29th May 1925; see ‘*Sada-e rusta khaiz*’, Ed. Khalil Ahmed Hamdi, p. 196. Philby’s article on Aqaba-Maan appeared in The Times, 29th June 1925. This too provided material for Abul ‘Ala for his article on the subject published in Jamiat, 6th August 1925. Like Philby, Abul ‘Ala favoured Abdul Aziz ibn Saud over the Sherifian clan.
76. Philby’s article ‘Palestine and Lord Balfour’, The Nineteenth Century and After, Vol. XCVII, June 1925, pp. 781-786.

77. 'Palestine and Lord Balfour: A reply by Israel Cohen', The Nineteenth Century and After, Vol. XCVIII, July 1925, p. 39.
78. Philby Archives, 6/5/3 1925-43; letter from Haji El Assil, May 1925.
79. Op.cit. Haneef Shahid, p. 171, citing the London Muslim House sermon, published in the Islamic Review, February 1919, Vol. 7, No. 2.
80. Ibid. pp. 190-191.
81. PRO FO371 5202 (1920); the quote is from a noted dated 5th March 1920, from the Director of Intelligence to the Under Secretary of State for Foreign Affairs.
82. The pledge cited was a declaration circulated by the Government of India in towns and villages in November 1914: "The Mussalmans of India should rest assured that nothing will be done by us or our Allies in this war which is likely to injure their religious feelings and sentiments. The holy places of Islam shall remain immune from molestation and every care will be taken to respect them. No operations will be conducted against the sacred seat of the Muslim Khilafat. We are only fighting the Turkish Ministers who are acting under the influence of Germany and not the Khalifa of Islam. The British Government not only on their behalf but also on behalf of their Allies take the responsibility of all these Pledges"; see 'The Khilafat and England', Syed Mahmud, 1921.
The Islamic Information Bureau published reports of meetings that protested on the way the pledge had been swept aside, including one addressed by Mohamed Ali Jinnah in London in March 1921: "We find this pledge is ruthlessly broken, and we find, to our great regret, that the British Premier has even gone to the extent of wriggling out of it. That shows that your statesmanship in this country is reaching the point of bankruptcy". See http://www.salaam.co.uk/knowledge/Islamic_news.pdf.
83. E.V. Gulbekian, 'A correspondence between Marmaduke Pickthall and the Armenian Bureau of London', Armenian Review, Autumn 1984, Vol. 37, No. 3; pp. 67-70.
84. Freemantle, Op.cit. p. 306-307.
85. Haneef Shahid, Op.cit. p. 293.
86. Jauhar remarked at the end of 1919 while in London, "There is the name of Islamic Bureau, but for all practical purposes it does not exist"; see Afzal Iqbal, 'The life and times of Mohamed Ali', Institute

of Islamic Culture, Lahore, 1974; p. 207. In the opinion of British Intelligence "…in November 1919 serious disputes.
87. PRO FO371 5202 (1920).
88. Haneef Shahid, Op.cit. p. 248-249, citing Islamic Review, January 1920, Vol. 8, No. 1, pp. 13-20.
89. The Times, 24th December 1919; other English Muslim signatories included Lady Zaynab Evelyn Cobbold.
90. Ibid. p. 249.
91. Ibid. p. 42, citing the Friday sermon published in Islamic Review, January 1921, Vol. 9, No. 1, pp. 11-20.
92. Freemantle, Op.cit. p. 314.
93. Op.cit. E.V. Gulbekian.
94. Op.cit. Afzal Iqbal; pp. 290-291.
95. see K.K Aziz's 'The Indian Khilafat Movement, 1915-1933' Pak Publishers, Karachi, 1972; p. 294.
96. Ibid. p. 280; the rumours that he had reverted to Islam in 1927 prompted the imam of the Ahmediyya Mosque in Southfield, A.R. Dard to write a congratulatory letter to his wife. Dora Philby noted at the back of this letter, 'My God, I hope this is not true'. Philby Papers, 6/5/4 ; The Philby Papers are deposited at Middle East Centre Archive, St. Antony's College, Oxford. The author is grateful to Debbie Usher, MEC Archivist for help in accessing the Papers.
97. PRO KV2/1119; File of H. St. John Philby.
98. Philby Papers, Box 6/6/3.
99. Monroe, op.cit. p. 181; describing Philby's expedition through the Rub-al Khali.
100. Monroe, Op.cit. pp. 33-34.
101. Philby Papers, Op.cit. Boxes 6/1/1 and 6/5/4/8. The 'London Mosque' was located at 63 Melrose Road, SW 18 and its imam at the time was A.R. Dard. The Times on 4th October 1926 reported that Faisal did not participate, and the following notice was put up on the premises: "Much against his own wishes the Emir has been forbidden to attend the ceremony". The following day The Times reported that "he was interdicted by his father [Abdul Aziz ibn Saud]".
102. PRO KV2/1119.
103. PRO KV2/119; letter from Sir David Petrie to Sir John E Shuckburgh, 7th May 1941.
104. PRO KV2/119; letter from Lord Lloyd to Harker, 27th November 1940.

105. Ibid; Special Branch report dated 12th June 1945. The report continues: "Philby's anti-British remarks provoked Ikbal Ali Shah into disclaiming responsibility for the views of the speaker and added that the meeting had not been called to discuss the wider aspects of the Arab question". Philby had expressed similar views in a letter to the Manchester Guardian published on 4th June 1945 in which he called for a bilateral Anglo-French agreement to renounce all special privileges in the Middle East accruing from the Sykes-Picot Agreement and to implement the McMahon promises of 1915 to the Arabs.
106. Philby, Forty Years in the Wilderness, Op.cit. pp. 68-69.
107. Muriel Pickthall, 'Personalia', in Haneef Shahid Op.cit; the article first appeared in Islamic Culture, Hyderabad, January 1937.
108. Ibid. p. 34; Pickthall's article in 'Islamic Review', July 1918, Vol. 6, No. 7.
109. Ibid. p. 170-171; Pickthall's article in 'Islamic Review', February 1919, Vol. 7, No. 2.
110. Pickthall, 'The Cultural Side of Islam', first lecture in the series he delivered in Madras in 1926. The edition consulted is published by Idara Isha'at-e-Diniyat, Delhi, 2007.
111. Haneef Shahid, Op.cit. p. 27.
112. Monroe, Op.cit. p. 152.
113. Philby, Forty Years in the Wilderness, Op.cit; p. 155.
114. Subsequent references from the Philby Archives, 6/5/4.
115. ibid; another invitee in a similar role was Dr A.J. Arberry; subsequent references to Philby's solidarity with Islamic bodies in Britain are also from the Philby Archives.
116. Reported in the Daily Sketch, 19th December 1942—"The Muslim Association invited me to the East London Mosque, Commercial Road, where about 400 Muslims of all nationalities gathered...dark-faced soldiers from overseas—Indians, Egyptians, West Africans, Persians, Arabs, and a few Free French crowded the room... afterwards curry and rice served in oblong dishes from which we all helped ourselves with a spoon apiece."
117. Philby Papers, Op.cit. 6/1/13, p. 19-20.
118. Haneef Shahid, Op.cit. p. 200.
119. Haneef Shahid, Op.cit. p. 188 & 195; the quote is from Pickthall's Eid-ul-Fitr Khutbah, June 1919.
120. Ibid.
121. Ibid. p. 174.
122. Ibid. p. 189.

123. Pickthall, The Cultural Side of Islam, Op.cit. p. 10.
124. Ibid. p. 33.
125. Ibid. p. 67.
126. Ibid. p. 129.
127. Ibid. pp. 50-51.
128. When they met in 1913 S'aid Halim Pasha thought Pickthall a 'charmant homme'; Pickthall saw him as "very neat, correct and automatic in his movements…they say he is a very honest and decent man, but not very brilliant". Haneef Shahid, Op.cit. p. 281; Syed Tanwir Wasti in 'Said Halim Pasha—Philosopher Prince', Middle Eastern Studies, Vol. 44, No. 1, pp. 85-104, January 2008, states that 'Islamlashmaq' was first published in 1918 in the magazine 'Sabeel ur-Reshad'.
129. Pickthall, The Cultural Side of Islam, Op.cit. p. 129.
130. Ibid. p. 141-143.
131. Ibid. p. 15; interestingly Pickthall did not include the 'ism' of Capitalism.
132. Professor Wasti notes, referring to *Javid Nama*: "In Iqbal's journey across the Heavens in the company of Rumi, the sage takes him to the sphere of Mercury where Iqbal—on whome the name conferred by Rumi is Zinda-Rud—hears the sound of the *adhan*….Rumi and Zinda-Rud then offer their prayers and, on proceeding further, they observe the spirits of Jamaluddin Afghani and Said Halim Pasha in prayer. The discourses of Afghani and Said Halim Pasha in this relatively short section of the Javid Nama quintessentially distill—in Iqbal's elegant Persian verse—the legacy and message of both Afghani and Said Halim Pasha". S.T. Wasti, 'Said Halim Pasha—Philosopher Prince', Middle Eastern Studies, Vol. 44, No. 1, January 2008; pp. 85-104; J.
133. Pickthall, The Cultural Side of Islam, Op.cit. p. 133.
134. Philby Papers, Op.cit. 6/1/10; from an article written by Philby entitled 'The Caliphate'; the date is not clear but could be 31st July 1938.
135. Philby Papers, 6/1/13 Op.cit. for this and subsequent quotes.
136. Evening Standard, 1st October 1943.
137. Philby, Forty Years in the Wilderness'; p. 126.
138. Ibid. p. 57.
139. Ibid. p. 156.
140. E.E. Speight in Haneef Shahid, Op.cit. p. 16.
141. Haneef Shahid, Op.cit. p. 137 citing Islamic Review, December 1918, Vol. 6, No. 12, pp. 429-431.